T0335301

"Grounded in both research and decades of ministry experiences, this book offers a much-needed guide to understand this spiritually curious generation. Weaving together data, stories, and practical application, Mark identifies the key shifts required to better engage this generation and to have fruitful spiritual conversations. *Faith for the Curious* is a must-read for ministry leaders and anyone trying to faithfully love unchurched friends today!"

Tom Lin, president and CEO, InterVarsity Christian Fellowship

"In Psalm 78 we read about the importance of passing our faith down to the next generations and telling them about God's glorious deeds, power, and wonders. I don't know of anyone who is better equipped and capable of helping the church do this than Mark Matlock. We must tell both the coming generations and the unchurched generations among us the good news of Jesus. In this book, you will discover not only information about where we are and the challenges we face but also hopeful and helpful ideas on what to do about them. Every one of us has a part in passing on our faith. Mark helps us do just that."

Ed Stetzer, PhD, dean, Talbot School of Theology,
Biola University

"*Faith for the Curious* is for anyone struggling to find effective ways to show and share the life they've found in Jesus in this challenging cultural moment. Drawing from his decades in student ministry leadership and pulling from thorough research on the Spiritually Curious among us, Mark gives us hope that there are paths forward—ways to better express the hope we have and ways to become more curious ourselves, for our own good. People are more open than we realize. Allow God to use this book to free you from fear and make you a light to many!"

Kevin Palau, president, Luis Palau Association

"Mark Matlock has done it again with his intellect, wit, insight, and insatiable desire to convert data into wisdom. In *Faith for the Curious* Mark helps us reframe curiosity as a source of energy to discover and cultivate faith in Jesus Christ. This is a must-read for anyone who hopes to shape the faith of the next generation."

Matt Markins, president and CEO, Awana; cofounder,
Child Discipleship Forum

"Mark Matlock's *Faith for the Curious* is an innovative exploration into the diverse landscape of American spirituality. Through the introduction of the Spiritually Curious and the Curious Skeptic, Matlock challenges traditional paradigms. As a leader striving to connect in an ever-changing world, I find this book to be an invaluable resource. It offers fresh perspectives on engaging those exploring Christianity, making it an essential read for anyone seeking to bridge the gap and foster meaningful conversations about faith in their everyday lives."

Rob Hoskins, president, OneHope

"Mark Matlock is a cultural expert who skillfully helps us to navigate the challenge of reaching the next generation spiritually. Instead of responding reactionarily, he gives us new tools to be proactive and ahead of the curve in an ever-evolving world. This book offers creative approaches, backed by solid data, to approach the curious not as enemies to be defeated but as treasures to be won."

Allen Yeh, professor of Intercultural Studies
and Missiology, Biola University

"There are spiritually curious people in your life and in mine. The question is, Will we be attentive and equipped to reach them? What I love about this book is that it is research-based, practical, and filled with stories of Mark practicing what he preaches. For the sake of the many spiritually curious people at your work and in your family, pick up a copy of *Faith for the Curious* and put it into practice."

Sean McDowell, PhD, professor of Apologetics,
Biola University; author, *Set Adrift*

"*Faith for the Curious* is a necessary resource for anyone seeking to understand the vast mission field before us. Mark has long been a trusted guide on the journey of discipleship, and this book does not disappoint."

Rev. Dr. Nicole Martin, founder and executive director,
Soulfire International Ministries

Faith for
the Curious

Faith for the Curious

How an Era of Spiritual Openness
Shapes the Way We Live
and Help Others Follow Jesus

MARK MATLOCK

BakerBooks

a division of Baker Publishing Group
Grand Rapids, Michigan

Published by Baker Books
a division of Baker Publishing Group
Grand Rapids, Michigan
BakerBooks.com

Printed in the United States of America

Library of Congress Cataloging-in-Publication Data
Names: Matlock, Mark, author.
Title: Faith for the curious : how an era of spiritual openness shapes the way we live and help others follow Jesus / Mark Matlock.
Description: Grand Rapids, Michigan : Baker Books, a division of Baker Publishing Group, [2024] | Includes bibliographical references.
Identifiers: LCCN 2024005421 | ISBN 9780801018718 (cloth) | ISBN 9781493444144 (ebook)
Subjects: LCSH: Non-church-affiliated people—United States. | Evangelistic work—United States.
Classification: LCC BR526 .M23 2024 | DDC 269/.20973—dc23/eng/20240226
LC record available at https://lccn.loc.gov/2024005421

Jacket design by Faceout Studio, Jeff Miller

Baker Publishing Group publications use paper produced from sustainable forestry practices and postconsumer waste whenever possible.

24   25   26   27   28   29   30   7   6   5   4   3   2   1

This book is dedicated to my children,
Dax and Skye,
and their friends who keep my faith fresh
through their curiosity.

Contents

Foreword

Maybe you've heard of Curious George (he's an illustrated monkey in children's books). And perhaps you know that curiosity kills the cat, though who knows why.

If curiosity is somehow connected to the animal kingdom, my friend Mark Matlock is the king of beasts. He is among the most curious people I know.

He is curious about people, striking up conversations with complete strangers with ease. He is fascinated by ideas—he's always got a new topic he's been reading about, listening to, exploring, and discussing.

He's also deeply interested in God. Mark has a unique way of thinking and communicating about theology, what people believe and why, and how believing in God makes life worth living.

Mark's inquisitive nature and desire to help people grow is why he is the perfect guide to help us understand the spiritually open moment we are experiencing in our society. Barna's social research since the pandemic shows most people are expressing much more openness and spiritual curiosity than they were before COVID hit. We are also seeing that teenagers around the world are open to God, open to spirituality, open to the Christian Scriptures, and open to Jesus.

In other words, spiritual curiosity is high right now. Our latest Barna research shows an unprecedented spiritual openness in the U.S. Get this: approximately three-quarters of adults in America say they believe in a higher power, and a majority say they're interested in exploring spirituality. That is good news for those who care about the gospel of Jesus taking root in hearts and minds!

Now, being open also means that people tend to be open to anything and everything. That can be mixed at best for those of us who believe in the essential and exclusive redemption that is offered by faith in Jesus.

This wonderful book is all about how the good kind of curiosity can help us to grow. *Faith for the Curious* provides a type of master class on how we as Christians can learn from those who are spiritually curious and help them become more alive to Jesus.

Perhaps you'd be interested to know how my twenty-five-year friendship with Mark helped to forge this book. Though we both attended Biola University, our paths didn't cross until a year or two after we had graduated. I was working for George Barna, and Mark was involved in youth ministry. One day, out of the blue, he called the company to see if George would be interested in doing a research project on teens and evangelism. His curiosity drove him to want to understand more deeply what was on the minds of teenagers. George agreed to do the study as long as Mark worked with me on it. I was new to the business, and my mentor was trying to help me get some easy wins on the scoresheet.

From this first project, Mark and I discovered that we shared a deep love for and curiosity about the next generation. We were still in our early twenties, but even as emerging adults, we could see the winds of culture shifting.

Since our initial Barna project, Mark has grown to be one of my closest friends. He went on to write many books, primarily for youth and student ministry leaders and parents, and I acquired Barna Group from George and Nancy in 2009. We continue to examine the spiritual journeys of young people as one of my company's key areas of research and subject matter expertise.

As such, Mark and I cowrote *Faith for Exiles*, which was published in 2019. We both were personally parenting our own teens and twentysomething children and were facing significant headwinds—society has become especially and insidiously faith-repellent. Our research showed that resilient faith was tougher to grow using the cultivation methods we relied on throughout the twentieth century. Professionally—and probably more urgently, personally—we needed some hopeful news and handrails to help guide our own kids and other young adults on how to cultivate a resilient faith. Together, Mark and I developed five research-based practices to help a new generation follow Jesus and thrive as exiles in digital Babylon.

Mark builds on all that work in this book, *Faith for the Curious*. He continues to weave the thread of reaching people and helping them grow in their faith in this current cultural moment. Massive receptivity to the possibility of God exists today. People want to believe in something bigger than themselves, a higher power to help them make sense of this messy world. We're living in a cultural moment full of enormous evangelistic opportunities.

Yet, as Mark soberly points out, the challenge facing Christians is whether we are ready and able to meet spiritually open people—where they are, as they are. Our data shows Christians and church leaders have significant work to do to bridge the trust gap for people who are spiritual but not religious.

Mark's work in *Faith for the Curious* is a major part of the bridge. In chapter after chapter, he provides relatable stories and experiences from his own life; data that tells the story of today's spiritually open people; and practical, concrete ideas for how to engage in spiritual conversations.

Mark authored this book under the Barna brand, which means he's included reliable charts, infographics, and statistics, and he unpacks them for those who share our love of a good data story. But this isn't your typical quantitative Barna research book. It's really about perception—seeing the world around us, understanding people's backstories and how they are connected to our Spiritually Open research (noted at the end of the book), and learning how to engage with people about their faith in a relevant, relatable way. Mark humbly shares his own journey as a high schooler who was quick to convince and less apt to be curious about others. Today, Mark is genuinely curious about people's spiritual journeys. He leans into every conversation ready to listen and learn about the person with whom he's talking.

Before you begin reading *Faith for the Curious*, I hope you'll pause for a moment and ask God to meet you where you are in your own faith life: to humbly ask him to soften your heart so it will be open and receptive to what you're about to experience in the pages that follow here. This book will help you be more curious about others, interested in ideas, and more open to God. Mark and I believe it will make you a better listener and, as such, even more open to receiving all that God has for you.

Yes, *Faith for the Curious* is an expression of Mark's expertise as a data storyteller. But it's also a narrative of his own evangelism journey, and it provides a much-needed modern-day guide for everyday Christians, pastors, and ministry leaders. Mark has made a great contribution to our team at Barna. As his friend and co-laborer in Christ, I could not more highly recommend this book to you. May you see and hear and act on the opportunities that abound to share Jesus now.

David Kinnaman
CEO, Barna

1

A New Way

*If she shows an openness to further exploration of faith, of
Jesus, what church can I recommend to her?*

The question rattled around in my head as I sat across
the table from Anika, an elegantly dressed, soft-spoken pro-
fessional with piercing blue eyes. It was my first time meeting her. Anika happened to be a dear friend of our mutual
acquaintance—an exuberant Irish New Yorker who often
interrogated me about my role as a minister and playfully
teased me about my ministry being a cult.

The three of us met with several friends in a charming coffee shop on the Upper East Side. Within mere minutes, our
conversation veered into matters of religion and spirituality—
once I was introduced as a "cult leader" by our mutual friend.
"Just for the record," I teased, "I'm never the one to bring my
Christianity into the conversation. You always mention it!"

It's not often that people delve into life's existential questions
with strangers, as much as some Christian apologists may want

us to believe that to be the case. Most people are too busy with bills, jobs, relationships, and other everyday concerns to spend much time pondering the meaning of life. However, Anika, a woman in her seventies, was coming to terms with the realization that she would likely attend more funerals than weddings with each passing year. She was at a point of transition, and it's at these moments when the "big questions" become more and more real. She seemed to be genuinely seeking answers.

Although she took this introduction to me as an opportunity to begin a spiritual conversation, I didn't have an agenda. I didn't try to rush in with answers to her questions and didn't play the role of "spiritual expert." That wouldn't have worked with her anyway.

At one point though, as her attention drifted into a contemplative gaze, she said something that lingered in the air—something that had clearly been weighing on her for a long time, possibly her whole life: "It would be nice to have something to believe in."

And so, our coffee meet-up evolved from a simple introduction into a sacred encounter: one of those remarkable moments when the boundaries between the physical and the eternal blurred. The spiritual realm was permeating the harsh realities of New York living. I stopped her in that moment. "Say more about that."

She continued, "It would be nice to believe there was something more, something bigger out there. A place where you knew you were going rather than just"—she made an end-of-life sound—"and that's it."

"Did you ever believe in anything?" I asked.

"Well, when I was a girl I was taught things, but I never really believed it."

"Is there a reason you don't believe in anything?" I asked.

"It just wasn't for me—all the rules, the talk about sin."

Again, I stopped her. "Anika, I'm going to go out on a limb because I'm sensing this is a really special moment. Could I share something about what I believe about sin and why I think you are talking to me about this? Would that be okay?"

She told me it was.

"I believe that God originally created us to be whole, completely fulfilled, flourishing, able to trust in him for everything we have. We weren't even capable of not trusting God; we were like mirrors that were able to reflect the image of God. We weren't God, but we were made in his image like the mirror."

"That's a beautiful image," she said.

"It is, but what happened is that this word you used, *sin*, shattered the mirror, breaking it into small pieces. I believe you have shards of that mirror inside you. It's God's image, and it wants to be bigger. I saw a little piece of that mirror when you said it would be nice to have something to believe in. Do you get that feeling often?"

I let her drive the conversation from that point. We talked for an hour, and as our conversation wrapped up, I asked her to pay attention to moments like that—moments where God's image might be bubbling to the surface of her soul. I asked her to make a mental note of those moments and see where they might lead. I also wanted to encourage her to find a church community where she could further explore her curiosity.

And that's where my own existential crisis about the church kicked in. The question at the beginning of this chapter—*If she shows an openness to further exploration of faith, of Jesus, what church can I recommend to her?*—haunted me.

It wasn't that I just couldn't envision the right church for her in New York City. After speaking in and traveling to more churches than I can count, I couldn't think of somewhere for her anywhere else in the country either. She wouldn't "fit" in the American church, which might be part of why Anika told me I was the first Christian who had engaged her in a way she found to be, in her words, "beautiful."

Anika didn't need a Sunday morning sermon. She didn't need an apologetics course, a primer on Christian doctrine, or for someone to explain who Jesus was. She didn't need a pamphlet, a Christian movie, or a website.

Anika had questions, to be sure, but they weren't intellectual questions. Not really. No, Anika had relationship questions about the experience of trusting God. She didn't want easy answers. She wanted someone to come alongside her on her spiritual exploration. She didn't want someone to talk *at* her. She wanted someone to talk *with* her.

Little could she have guessed how often God himself shows up when two people sit down to talk about him honestly and humbly.

Maybe sitting with God for a while would help her figure out if she could trust him the way I did. She'd experienced a lot of life in New York and needed a guide into the thin space between a life of struggle under the sun and one that enters into a relationship with God through his Son.

What Would a Pastor Do?

I've grown comfortable talking with people who have no thoughts about or opinion of Christianity, primarily through the friendships my kids have made with non-Christians. While my ministry work almost completely sheltered me from the unchurched for decades, my children—who are bent toward the arts—have always been in friend groups with people who were not "the youth group type" that I had spent most of my life ministering to as a youth pastor. By getting to know my kids' friends, I not only learned a lot about them, I learned a lot about the way we as Christians approach people like them—and why we often let them down.

It wasn't uncommon for my kids' friends to ask for an invitation to dinner just to talk to me. They were curious about what I did for a living. Most of them hadn't encountered adults who were easy to engage with honestly and authentically about faith, and contrary to popular opinion, these kids were intrigued by the opportunity. From their perspective, I was a middle-aged cisgender male who had an appreciation for art but was vocationally a minister. They weren't so much curious about me as they were curious about what I believed in and thought about different topics. Unlike Anika, they weren't necessarily interested in answers to life's big existential questions. But they wondered what I thought about different social issues, justice causes, and news events that had a direct impact on their daily lives. They wondered how my beliefs as a Christian influenced my perspective on things happening in their world. While most of them would have labeled themselves atheist, agnostic, or none, they were all curious . . . spiritually curious.

Causing me to wonder, *Does the church know how to engage curious people?*

I first introduced this idea of spiritual curiosity while hosting a tour of twenty-six cities for The Seed Company in 2017. We were sharing research insights to help pastors know how to help expand their church's awareness of Bible translation and world mission. Research done by American Bible Society was also presented on this tour to help pastors understand barriers to the Bible. The hope was to help pastors discover more opportunities to increase Bible reading among both people in their churches and people outside them.

As we workshopped the research's insights about the Spiritually Curious with pastors, I realized that many of the pastors were struggling. Applying this research in practical ways was difficult for them because, according to our studies, it's not enough to simply provide easy answers to spiritually curious people. This approach might seem effective, but it leaves spiritually curious people unsatisfied. Spiritually curious people want something more, and many of the pastors in the workshop didn't have a framework for understanding how a curious person wants to explore spiritual themes and practices. This surprised me.

Example: if a person showed curiosity about what the Bible has to say about dinosaurs (one of the top twenty most frequently searched questions about the Bible on Google, by the way!), most pastors in our workshops said they would write a sermon series about dinosaurs, the Bible, and maybe the Genesis account of creation.

Now, sermons on what the Bible says about dinosaurs might be interesting, well-researched, and skillfully preached. But they can't be a Socratic dialogue that engages the questions of the Spiritually Curious along the way:

- Why are you curious about what the Bible says about dinosaurs? Is there a question behind the question?
- What do you believe about the Bible as a spiritual document?

- What are your trusted sources of truth?
- What might change in the world if you could answer this question?
- Might there be other views Christians hold on how to interpret this?

Sermons are great. I've learned a great deal from sermons in my life and I've written more than I care to count. But we need to be aware of both their uses and their limitations. Sermons are a one-way monologue where a group of people are willingly taking the time to learn from someone they trust. The Spiritually Curious aren't necessarily ready for that kind of engagement. They're looking for a two-way conversation that can veer in different directions.

The curious want more of a tour guide or a museum docent. They want someone who offers opportunities for feedback, engagement, and support as they experience specific subject matter. In fact, the museum environment is both an apt metaphor and a useful model for churches to consider if seeking to more effectively engage the Spiritually Curious.

Visiting a Museum

Museum exhibits are curated experiences. If you're going to an exhibit on van Gogh, for instance, you're probably not going to see his entire body of work. Nor will you sit and listen to someone tell you everything they think you need to know about him for thirty minutes. Instead, you'll see pieces that have been hand-selected to illuminate a particular time in his life or theme in his work. Each curated piece is displayed in a particular order to create a journey that tells a story about the subject matter at hand.

Exhibits employ different sensory aspects—lighting, sound, video, and sometimes immersive and hands-on opportunities—to further draw people into the learning experience. Wall placards, an audio guide narrating the experience, a docent giving a guided tour—museums make sure people have multiple options for interacting with and experiencing their content.

Museums understand there's no one-size-fits-all approach. Everyone goes at their own pace and engages with the material in their own way. Some will choose to skip over parts of the exhibit that don't seem interesting. Others might sit and stare at one piece until they've explored all the nuances of it. A museum allows you a self-guided experience, an opportunity to focus on what is most interesting to you. While the path is directed, it's often nonlinear, allowing the visitor to spend as much time as they want in an area of their choosing (although there can be timed exhibits and opening and closing hours).

Museums also don't typically limit who can come to exhibits; anyone who buys a ticket is welcome. People who think van Gogh was a genius are welcome, of course. But so are people who find him problematic or boring or irrelevant. No matter what attitude someone brings to the material, museums provide a nonjudgmental environment to challenge those assumptions and reward further exploration. No matter what attitude you bring into a museum, you leave enriched, knowing more than you did when you arrived. Museums are designed to spark, engage, and satisfy the curiosity of all who seek out the experience.

Imagine taking a group of middle school students to a museum exhibit featuring art from the twentieth century. If you simply set them loose, many would go through the whole thing in about ten minutes, learning little if anything.

But what if, in the weeks before the visit, you'd been able to tell them a little about what they would be seeing? Maybe you'd even have them choose three artists whose works they needed to find on their museum visit. What if you'd given them an opportunity to paint something themselves before they went—maybe to copy a painting by Piet Mondrian (without telling them they were reproducing a well-known work they'd be seeing)? What if they had an assignment at the end of the trip to recreate a painting they saw?

Think about how having that information prior to entering the museum would change their experience.

In addition, now imagine that rather than being set loose, each middle schooler gets a one-on-one guide to interact with while touring the exhibit. This guide can help direct their attention to what they might be overlooking, assist them with any portions that they aren't understanding, and provide contextual background to enrich their understanding of what they're seeing.

Then, when the visit is over, they come back on the bus and get to share what they saw and how it impacted them. Their classmates also get to learn a little about what they saw from the perspective of one of their peers.

Christians do this on mission trips all the time (when we do them well). We prepare for the trip, anticipating what is coming. We provide support and feedback while on the trip. And then afterward, we debrief. Maybe that's why mission trips, service projects, and summer camps have exponential spiritual impact. We are engaging in a holistic experience that leverages a person's curiosity.

And yet, since that 2017 Seed Company tour, I've been grappling with a difficult question: Do those of us who want others to come to Christ truly understand how to reach this group of people, the Spiritually Curious? Are we willing to adjust our ways of thinking and doing things in order to reach them?

Prodigals

When I helped Barna Group CEO David Kinnaman analyze and frame the research for his book *You Lost Me* in 2010, I was fascinated with the profile of those we came to call Prodigals.

Prodigals are "ex-Christians"—individuals who once identified as Christians but no longer do. It isn't just that they've left the church, they've left their faith behind too. At that time, Prodigals made up about 11 percent of the individuals ages eighteen to twenty-nine that we surveyed. (That number would jump to 22 percent less than a decade later when we surveyed the same age range for *Faith for Exiles*.)[1]

Often, when Christians think about people like this, they have an image of an angry, cynical know-it-all who is just itching for a theological debate. We tend to think that these Prodigals are bitter and resentful and selfishly want to bring other Christians down to their level. We may use words like *exvangelical* or *deconstructing* almost as a warning, to caution other Christians against following that same path.

However, looking deeper at the Prodigals, I found that they didn't match the picture of the anti-Christian intellectual wanting to debate and destroy the believers of the Christian faith. There were usually two reasons why these individuals left faith and the church.

First, they had been hurt by someone in the church or the sum collective of the church. They'd put their trust in a Christian or maybe a church, and they'd been betrayed, hurt, or even abused. Maybe they turned to the church in a time of need and found their concerns dismissed or belittled. Maybe they'd been hurt by someone in the church, and the church itself was more interested in protecting its reputation than in protecting them. Many of these people were angry or mad at the church, but more out of hurt and less out of intellectual disagreement.

Second was a group of people who decided that they just didn't believe the tenets of the faith anymore. Some had stronger reasons and feelings than others, but, surprisingly, most still held positive views of the church and their parents. Some even noted that they waited until college to leave the faith because they didn't want to hurt their parents. One Prodigal told me they wished they could believe, but they just couldn't. I'm glad David chose to label this group Prodigals, because it's more hopeful than *atheists* or *ex-Christians*.

We often expect nonbelievers to be hard-core atheists like Madalyn Murray O'Hair or Richard Dawkins, who aren't just atheists but anti-Christian with an almost militant nature. We take an unhealthy us versus them approach, where those who aren't with us must be against us. We assume most atheists and agnostics are smug elitists who are mocking believers behind our backs when they aren't doing it to our faces.

But Barna's research says this simply isn't the reality. After looking at the Prodigals and matching that data with my own experiences with non-Christians, I began calling this the age of "polite atheism." These people choose disbelief in God but are okay with others believing something else . . . and often have an appreciation for those who do. Their disbelief also doesn't mean that they aren't open to discussing their journey or that they aren't still searching for greater meaning.

The Spiritually Curious

I have two aims for this book, and they will interweave through the subsequent chapters. The first is to help us understand who the Spiritually Curious are in a deeper way. This large and growing group of Americans is open to the world beyond their five senses and eager to explore their questions about the spiritual realm among a safe, nonjudgmental group of fellow travelers and guides. These people differ from each other in many ways, but curiosity is always a distinguishing factor that draws them together. As a church leader or a person interested in connecting people to Jesus, I hope you want to learn ways to better engage this group and meet their needs by seizing the opportunities that this era of spiritual openness brings.

The second goal is to help us make a shift in the way we are personally and collectively practicing Christianity. We have a lot to gain from becoming more curious ourselves, from realizing there may be something we are missing in our own spiritual life that needs tending to, and from embracing the idea that we can't take people somewhere we haven't been.

Spiritual curiosity isn't a fire to be extinguished; it's a garden to be cultivated. Gardening takes a lot more time and energy than putting out a fire. You've got to water some plants, prune others, and uproot when necessary. It's a serious undertaking. It takes a lot of patience. It's a little risky. But the results can be beautiful.

We'll be diving into some territory and asking questions that may at times be uncomfortable. We are leaving the shore, and the waters may get a little choppy. All I ask is that you tune up your own sense of curiosity as you read. Even if you don't agree with me on every single point, I hope you can remain engaged. That's part of what curiosity is all about. From the spiritually curious teens my kids would bring home to the older "Anikas" who would find it difficult to find a church that will meet them at their level, it's clear we have a lot of work to do. If we're serious about reaching those who stand outside the faith but are curious about it, we need to be able to meet them where they are on their journey. Are you ready to get started?

2

The Spiritually Curious

In the late nineties, a remarkable phenomenon known as "crossing over" began to take hold in the Contemporary Christian Music world, propelled by bands like Jars of Clay and DC Talk. Music artist Amy Grant had already pioneered a Christian path to mainstream success by mixing catchy, bubbly pop songs into her mix of more traditionally spiritual tunes. Now a new generation was picking up her torch and carrying it even further, crafting real hits that sounded right at home on Top 40 charts and MTV without sacrificing their distinct Christian identity. These new acts found themselves increasingly embraced by a broader demographic, and they started playing to bigger audiences. The release of Michael W. Smith's 2001 worship album (appropriately titled *Worship*) coupled with the surging popularity of Third Day revolutionized how the music industry perceived the potential of Christian artists.

As the landscape rapidly evolved, bands faced crucial decisions about the kind of music they wanted to make. The music industry realized that there was a much larger market for these "spiritual" records than previously imagined. Larger secular entities started acquiring smaller Christian record labels, hoping to find the next DC Talk or Jars of Clay. It was a complicated time for newer, younger Christian bands. The shifting tides of acceptance and market dynamics compelled artists to navigate uncharted territory. Christian musicians were rethinking what it could mean to be a "Christian band" and were redefining the boundaries of their musical influence.

At that time a small, unknown band called MercyMe was traveling with me. WisdomWorks, a ministry I founded, managed them from our garage office in Irving, Texas. They were primarily worship artists on the precipice of a huge decision—whether to go secular or stay sacred. We had sold thirty thousand copies of MercyMe's self-produced album *The Worship Project* from our garage. One day our staff of two woke up to hear that one of MercyMe's songs was being played on The Wolf, a secular station in the Dallas area at the time. By the time we tuned in our radios, the DJ was saying, "Stop calling. We will play the song again."

That song was "I Can Only Imagine." It was the most overtly Christian song one could play on a secular station at the time. It's a song about heaven and what Christians believe awaits them. Here's a sample lyric: "Surrounded by your glory, what will my heart feel? Will I dance for you, Jesus? Or in awe of you be still?"

And those listening to this station, which regularly featured guys like Eminem and 50 Cent, were asking to hear

"I Can Only Imagine" again and again. At that moment, I realized that America is a much more Christian nation than I had assumed.

Eventually, MercyMe's debut studio album *Almost There*, which featured "I Can Only Imagine," went platinum. I took a couple weeks to tour with the band. We made stops across America and even took a private plane in the middle of the tour to do a couple of television spots in New York for some major morning news programs. It was amazing to meet all the people moved by this song. The song's biggest fans came not only from inside the church but outside it as well.

Nobody knew or cared who I was, so this gave me great cover to meet the people standing in line to meet the band. Sometimes it was the hair and makeup person or the camera operator who I got to interact with. On *Good Morning America*, one director said MercyMe's appearance had caused more excitement in the building than a well-known singer who had appeared the day before.

What was going on here?

Defining Our Terms

In recent years I've had the privilege of being a presenter and workshop facilitator for Barna, a research and communications company that studies faith and culture. As a senior Barna Fellow, I've partnered with them on several research projects and coauthored a book, *Faith for Exiles*, with Barna's CEO David Kinnaman. This has allowed me a front-row seat as Barna has been looking at faith beliefs and practices, particularly in the U.S. For nearly forty years they've tracked what Christians and non-Christians believe, and there is no question: while Christianity remains vibrant in the U.S., participation in our churches is dropping fast. In 1993, 45 percent of U.S. adults attended church weekly, but as of our current study, it's just 21 percent.[1]

Nonetheless, most people generally think of themselves as Christian. At present, 64 percent of the general U.S. population still identifies as Christian when asked about faith beliefs in Barna surveys. This percentage shocked me at first because it runs counter to my own experience, and likely to yours as well. In broader culture and in personal interactions, I don't often have the sense that I am in the majority as a Christian. Rather, it can feel like my devout faith life is unusual or met with a raised eyebrow. There is good reason that I and many other faithful Christians might feel that way. First, while most Americans still self-identify as Christian, you can see Christian identity is in fact on the decline over time and across generations.

The biggest shift in religion has been the number of people who are opting out altogether. You've likely heard this group referred to as the Nones. These people don't claim any label for their spiritual beliefs or lack thereof. They don't claim any religion, but they don't always like being called an atheist or agnostic either. This cohort is young and is challenging older Christians like me to consider new ways of thinking about the Christian faith and those people who are outside and adjacent to it.

If we look closely at Gen Z respondents, breaking them down into teens (aged thirteen to seventeen) and young adults (aged eighteen to twenty-two), we see the percentage of those who identify as atheist, agnostic, or of no faith is

Christian Identity Is on the Decline—and "Nones" Are on the Rise

● Christian   Other faith ● Atheist ○ Agnostic ● No faith

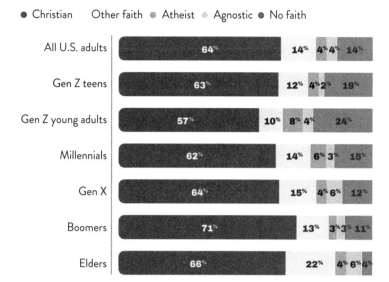

	Christian	Other faith	Atheist	Agnostic	No faith
All U.S. adults	64%	14%	4%	4%	14%
Gen Z teens	63%	12%	4%	2%	19%
Gen Z young adults	57%	10%	8%	4%	24%
Millennials	62%	14%	6%	3%	15%
Gen X	64%	15%	4%	6%	12%
Boomers	71%	13%	3%	3%	11%
Elders	66%	22%	4%	6%	4%

n=2,005 U.S. teens and adults, December 13–22, 2022. Source: Barna Group

trending upward among this cohort. Research from Barna shows that quick, decisive shifts away from religion in general and Christianity in particular seem to occur as this next generation is emerging into early adulthood. (Here I should add that when you see *n*= with each chart, it refers to the sample size: the number of people who responded to the questionnaire.)

What's more, among the considerable two-thirds of the U.S. population who still identify with Christianity, we have to acknowledge that this identification does not necessarily align with actual religious practices. In other words, *Christian* might be the word they use to describe themselves, but whether their actual belief and behavior line up with a traditional understanding of Christianity is another matter altogether.

To gain a more nuanced understanding, Barna employs specific measures to identify the 20 percent of Americans who not only claim Christian affiliation but also actively practice and value their faith. Astonishingly, nearly two-thirds of those who call themselves Christian do not meet this definition of a "Practicing Christian"; they do not regularly attend church or even consider religious faith to be an important part of their lives. This understanding sheds light on the complex dynamics at play within the Christian landscape of America.

The research shows that those Nonpracticing Christians bear little resemblance in belief or practice to the Christianity presented in the Scriptures, regardless of how they may self-identify. In fact, their responses often look more like those of non-Christians than Practicing Christians.

Two in Five U.S. Adults Are Nonpracticing Christians

● Practicing Christians　● Nonpracticing Christians　● Non-Christians

All U.S. adults	20%	38%	42%

Only one in five U.S. adults meet all of the following criteria:
1. Identify as Christian
2. Attend church monthly
3. Strongly agree their religious faith is very important in their life today

n=1,890 U.S. adults, December 13–22, 2022. Source: Barna Group

For that reason, we will often look at the contrast between Practicing Christians and the rest of the U.S. population, combining Nonpracticing Christians and those who identify as None or something else. This group—Nonpracticing Christians combined with Nones—is the audience we want to understand so that we can more effectively reach them with the Good News of Jesus Christ.

What Is Spiritual Curiosity?

My daughter's AP art class was hosting Parent Critique Day, a time when parents could come in and take part in the peer critiques of the recent work done by the class. Having taken many art classes in college myself, I was familiar with this process and was curious to see the work of other students. As a parent, you always love what your kid makes, but to see their work up against the work of other kids, well, that was something I was curious to experience. I came in ready for anything. My only goal was to not embarrass my daughter, which *is* the goal most of the time.

Even though we lived in the Bible Belt, most of my daughter Skye's classmates were not Christians. And though most of my life's work has been ministering to teenagers, her friends didn't know this. They just knew me as "a pastor."

The critique went well. I was impressed with the quality of work these students had put out and felt good about my daughter's decision to pursue a career in fashion design. The next day Skye asked if some of her friends could come over for dinner. "They want to meet you and talk to you. They actually think you are kind of interesting."

This surprised her, and, of course, I welcomed them into my home.

They had loads of questions about my creative experiences and also about my vocation as a pastor. They were curious about faith and what that looked like. The idea that a grown-up might be interested in both faith and creativity was a novel thing. I realized that my background in art and the creative fields was something they hadn't encountered in an adult who spoke their language. Over time, I got to know these friends. I became the dad who took all the kids to the clubs down in the Deep Ellum area of Dallas to hear their favorite bands. We would go out and talk over a Whataburger on the way home.

These were really smart teenagers, and most of them didn't have a clue about faith and had never considered how it might intersect with the arts. Through my conversations with them, I saw a spiritual curiosity that felt different from interactions I'd had with non-Christians in the past. Through conversations, these teenagers started to open up to a way of thinking about faith that was new and exciting to them. What is more, there was a growing pool of "de-churched" teens who had rejected a form of Christianity that Jesus probably would have rejected too. But given their lack of guidance, they didn't know there was a way to practice Christianity in church that felt much more like Jesus.

In preparation for writing this book, I met with David John Seel, author of *The New Copernicans*, to discuss the Spiritually Curious. Here's what he said:

Right now the church's crisis is that we do not know how to translate our faith to the next generation. The next generation is not going to put up with the way we've communicated faith in the past. They are a post-Enlightenment generation. And it is true that they are more spiritually open. They're haunted. The secular media likes to think of the rise of religious Nones as a sign of growing secularity or atheism. And of course that's not true. It's the rise of an alternative form of spirituality. In fact, they're more spiritually oriented than their predecessors. And they are haunted by the fear of missing out.

I see spiritual curiosity on a continuum. "Haunted" is a state of emotional and/or spiritual unrest with the sense that there's got to be something larger than themselves, some meaning, and their view of reality is one with skylights, not a world without windows. It's a world with windows. The problem is they're clueless about what's beyond the skylight. And they're curious about what is beyond. Now for me, "haunted" is a static state of restlessness; "curious" is somebody who's beginning to ask questions, but not quite a seeker.[2]

Let me try to draw a picture of what I think is going on:

There are two axes—one that measures the extremes of a person's curiosity and the other that looks at their spiritual worldview.

Along the horizontal x-axis we have a person's worldview as it relates to the supernatural realm. At one extreme is a belief in a supernatural world of some kind, and at the other is a belief that only the physical world exists. A series of questions helped us identify where people were along the spectrum.

What has shifted—as we have come into a post-Enlightenment, postmodern, post-Christian, post-truth, well,

Supernaturalism x Curiosity

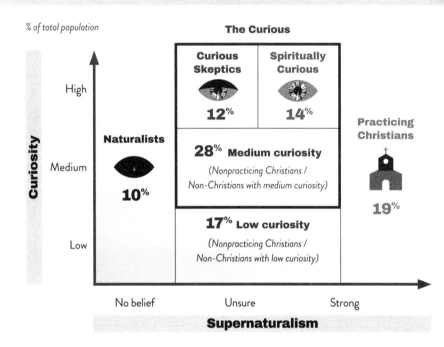

% of total population

The Curious

Curiosity

| | Curious Skeptics | Spiritually Curious |

High — Curious Skeptics **12%** / Spiritually Curious **14%**

Naturalists 10%

Medium — **28%** Medium curiosity (*Nonpracticing Christians / Non-Christians with medium curiosity*)

Practicing Christians 19%

Low — **17%** Low curiosity (*Nonpracticing Christians / Non-Christians with low curiosity*)

Supernaturalism: No belief — Unsure — Strong

The Spiritually Curious

These are adults who are not part of the Christian church (meaning, they are non-Christians or Nonpracticing Christians), yet they believe there is a real spiritual dimension and show high levels of curiosity.

The Curious Skeptics

These non-Christians and Nonpracticing Christians also show high levels of curiosity. When it comes to spirituality, big questions loom; they are uncertain if there is a spiritual dimension, or they believe there is no way to know for sure.

The Naturalists

Some people are pretty much closed off to the idea of there being a spiritual realm. Here, we're referring to those who identify as having no faith and are at least somewhat certain there is no spiritual dimension and no afterlife. Instead, they tend to say the physical world is all there is. But don't assume Naturalists lack general curiosity; 30 percent exhibit a high level.

n=525 U.S. adults who are Nonpracticing Christians or non-Christians, February 19–23, 2023. Source: Barna Group

A Spectrum of Spiritual Views

Some people say there is nothing more to this world than what we can taste, touch, hear, see, and smell. Others say there's a spiritual or supernatural dimension that is just as real as the physical world. What do you think there is?

- There is a real spiritual dimension ● There is no way to know this
- I am not sure ● The physical world is all there is

| All U.S. adults | 47% | 25% | 16% | 12% |

n=1,501 U.S. adults, February 19–23, 2023. Source: Barna Group

post-everything world—is that the strong, rational, scientific mind has been tempered with a basic need to validate from experience whether something actually works.

The y-axis is a little more complicated. With the right questions, it's not too hard to calculate just how much a person might believe in the supernatural. But how do we measure curiosity and openness?

Numerous studies have been conducted on the subject of curiosity, with several researchers offering their insights. One of the first psychologists to develop a model of curiosity was Daniel Berlyne.

Berlyne suggested that curiosity seeking helps us find a happy medium between two uncomfortable states—understimulation and overstimulation. When we're bored, we employ "diversive curiosity" to find something that will grab our attention. Conversely, when we're overwhelmed, we employ "specific curiosity" to make sense of the situation and find some level of understanding. A kid who spends math class wondering what it'd be like to fly is using diversive curiosity. A person lost in the woods who tries to find True North is using specific curiosity.[3]

George Loewenstein contributed to this work by creating the "information-gap" theory in a 1994 paper for the *Psychological Bulletin* titled "The Psychology of Curiosity."[4] This theory suggests that we activate curiosity when we feel like there's a gap in our knowledge or understanding that we need to fill. This lack of knowledge is like an itch that needs to be scratched. Curiosity is the act of scratching that itch.

Edward Deci is another individual who refined the concept of curiosity. In the 1970s, he argued that we're not just curious to avoid negative sensations; we're also motivated to seek out positive stimulation. We want to push ourselves to explore, learn, and grow; to seek novelty and challenges; and to stretch our abilities. Anytime a person picks up a new hobby, masters a new skill, or explores a new subject, they are ultimately exercising curiosity.

These and other concepts led to the development of the Curiosity and Exploration Inventory, a two-factor model of curiosity[5] (recently expanded to a five-factor model), by Dr. Todd Kashdan's team of researchers.

Kashdan's Curiosity and Exploration Inventory uses two factors—"stretching" and "embracing"—to measure the curiosity in others. "Stretching" is the motivation to seek out new information and experiences. "Embracing" is a willingness to welcome the uncertain and unpredictable nature of everyday life. Stretching is the interest in learning. Embracing is understanding that learning might take you past your comfort zone.

When the Barna team and I came together to develop the research for this book, I knew I wanted to use some of these

The Curiosity Scale

Based on their responses to 10 items, people were scored in terms of their motivation to seek out the new and their willingness to embrace the uncertain.

● High curiosity   ● Moderate curiosity   ○ Low curiosity

All U.S. adults | **38%** | **38%** | **24%**

Read each of the following statements and decide how much you agree with each according to your beliefs and experiences.
% strongly agree

○ All U.S. adults

I actively seek as much information as I can in new situations	**31%**
I view challenging situations as an opportunity to grow and learn	**23%**
I frequently seek out opportunities to challenge myself and grow as a person	**19%**
Everywhere I go, I am out looking for new things or experiences	**18%**
I am always looking for experiences that challenge how I think about myself and the world	**18%**
I am at my best when doing something that is complex or challenging	**17%**
I am the kind of person who embraces unfamiliar people, events, and places	**15%**
I am the type of person who really enjoys the uncertainty of everyday life	**11%**
I prefer jobs that are excitingly unpredictable	**10%**
I like to do things that are a little frightening	**7%**

n=1,501 U.S. adults, February 19–23, 2023. Source: Barna Group

measures of curiosity. Combining principles and questions from the theories I've mentioned, we surveyed people about traits like their desire for new information or experiences, or their relationship to unpredictability or unfamiliarity.

We were then able to score respondents along a spectrum of high, moderate, and low curiosity to cull those who are curious.

We'll build on these themes throughout this book and use the data to spotlight other ways curiosity shows up. This methodology gives us at least a starting point to begin exploring engagement with people more broadly as we seek to bring the Good News to people in a broken world.

Profiles of the Curious (and Not So Curious)

We scored all respondents using these measures, and found these distinct profiles.

The Curious

Fifty-four percent of non-Christians and Nonpracticing Christians showed mid to high curiosity. That's a significant chunk of the population. Initially this group was the focus of our research, but when we applied their belief in the supernatural, we started seeing two stronger profiles emerge: the Curious Skeptic and the Spiritually Curious. While the medium curiosity group bears resemblance to these two profiles, we found that culling them out helped us understand the nuances between the groups. What does this mean? Simply this: in an era of open spirituality, people's beliefs are fluid. Know that the curious population is large, and we can use what we learn about the Spiritually

Curious and Curious Skeptic to reach out to all who are curious.

The Spiritually Curious

The Spiritually Curious, by our definition, are those who believe there is a supernatural realm. This not only includes non-Christians but also Nonpracticing Christians. I feel many in this group may need little more than an introduction to the dynamics of a spiritual life in Christ to cross the chasm to a life of faith in Jesus. They are open to learning more and accepting of new ideas. However, it's likely we are missing the opportunities to engage this group because we do not approach them with the right posture of intellectual or experiential humility. As open as the Spiritually Curious might be to Christian teaching, they are turned off by simplistic answers or cookie-cutter responses to their thoughtful, personal questions.

This group responds well to empathy, as they experience loneliness, anxiety, and a deep feeling of being overwhelmed in life. Simple bumper-sticker responses that are not sensitive and relationally engaging to their felt needs will be a conversation ender.

Curious Skeptics

This group exhibits high curiosity, but it's a curiosity rooted in skepticism. Curious Skeptics aren't sure what to believe about the supernatural realm or if anything can be known for certain about its existence, but that doesn't mean they aren't interested in hearing other opinions on the matter. Traditional apologetics—with a focus on intellectual objections to Christianity, such as the problem of evil or historical evidence—can be engaging to this group. But more than likely, apologetics on their own won't be enough. More will be required to engage the openness this group displays. A lack of intellectual humility on the part of any person or church trying to connect with them will be the greatest barrier to reaching this group.

Naturalists

Naturalists are certain in their belief that what we experience with our five senses is all there is to experience. They are closed to the idea that there is a supernatural realm.

This segment of the population makes up nearly 10 percent of respondents—the rough equivalent of about twenty-five million people (among the more than 250 million U.S. adults).

It's likely that a majority of our current apologetic efforts have been spent responding to this group though. A considerable amount of the church's time and resources have gone toward attempting to convince the world that the spiritual realm is real. And yet, according to our research, very few people need to be convinced of that! In the late 1920s, Christians were concerned that the Scopes Monkey Trial would pave the way for an ascendance of naturalism in America, but the last century has not seen a significant drop in the number of people who believe in the supernatural realm. By and large, Americans believe there is more to life than what is experienced with our five senses.

While we will occasionally reference the Naturalist and Curious Skeptic, the Spiritually Curious are the primary focus of this book. We will be contrasting their beliefs, experiences, and preferences with Practicing Christians, who make up most of our regular church attendees today.

The Spiritually Curious

Now that we know our key population segments and some of their characteristics, let's begin our deep dive into the Spiritually Curious. I'll introduce eight qualities of the Spiritually Curious here, and we'll continue to unpack them as we sit with this open-minded group.

1. The Spiritually Curious do not have strong opinions about the supernatural but believe it exists.

Forty-seven percent of Americans are certain there is a spiritual or supernatural dimension to life. Isn't that remarkable? While they may not attribute the unseen to deity of any kind (think psychic energy or particle physics), they know there is something more. Ecclesiastes 3 says God has placed "eternity in the human heart" (v. 11). By our definition, 100 percent of the Spiritually Curious believe there is a supernatural existence.

2. The Spiritually Curious are open to experiences and experiments related to the spiritual.

Spiritually curious people are ready to explore. There are thousands of spiritual retreats, seminars, and workshops that offer the promise of significant breakthroughs. People want an opportunity to "try on" something in a concentrated but noncommittal way, as they are open to new ways of thinking and approaches to life.

3. The Spiritually Curious are less inclined to be open to institutional religious experiences.

For better or worse, traditional institutional experiences of the church are less interesting. This may be caused by the fact that they have become too familiar, even to those who have never tried them. They're not particularly curious about "organized religion" because they think they've seen most of what it has to offer. Additionally, "church" has quite a bit of baggage associated with it through scandal and bad press. The Spiritually Curious may be deterred from more deeply exploring "church" because they or people close to them have been hurt by the institution.

4. The Spiritually Curious need safety around doubts and questions.

People have access to incredible information today. Through the internet and social media, they can ask their most personal questions without judgment, shame, or risk of humiliation. A key takeaway we first unpacked in *Faith for Exiles* is a simple fact of the modern age: Screens *disciple*. And as AI and other new technologies emerge, people will increasingly rely on the privacy of their own screens to seek the answers they're looking for.

Sometimes I'll ask the young people I work with what their search history looks like. This is obviously a question that invites a lot of vulnerable responses. As they share the kinds of questions they're asking online, I've come to realize that they are asking questions I will never get the opportunity to help them answer unless they feel safe sharing them with me. We need the church to be a place where people can safely bring their questions and doubts. If we want people to trust our answers, we first have to assure them they are safe to ask their questions.

5. The Spiritually Curious want more intensity in their experiences, not less.

This one surprised me. Often we try to make people's gateway into spiritual experiences as inoffensive and accessible as possible. We go to great lengths to make church feel casual and strip away anything that might feel too "religious" or "traditional." While there is nothing wrong with using empathy to think about how others experience spirituality, there's a sense among the Spiritually Curious that they want the real deal, not something watered down or filtered. It's safe to say that the Spiritually Curious get enough "casual" in everyday life. If they're coming to church, they want real, unabridged church. So while experiences need to be carefully considered, we need to trust that God will meet each person where they are.

6. The Spiritually Curious see spiritual matters as less existential and more practical than you might expect.

Most people aren't asking the big questions of life as much as we would like to believe. Issues like the meaning of life and what happens when we die are not as "top of mind" for these people as they were for, say, Saint Augustine or Søren Kierkegaard. This doesn't mean these questions aren't important, but most people are first looking to solve practical problems. They are looking to solve issues related to finances, relationships, and health—the day-to-day—more than they are looking to find meaning and significance. Thankfully, the

Christian faith offers wisdom for both arenas. If the church can show these people how relevant Jesus's teachings are to their most immediate concerns, they may then be more inclined to trust its answers to the big questions.

7. The Spiritually Curious understand Jesus more by how he behaved as a historical or mythological figure than as a means to salvation.

In our research on people's perceptions of Jesus, they are far less likely than Practicing Christians and pastors to identify Jesus as King or Savior and much more as a teacher, a person of compassion, or one who stands against injustice or forgave those who wronged him. These descriptors are much less likely chosen by pastors and Christians, which tells us, when we are introducing the Spiritually Curious to Jesus, we should be aware of their frame of reference. They deeply admire Jesus and likely wish more people would take his teachings on kindness and compassion to heart. They may even be open to acknowledging that they don't always live up to his example. But they are less likely to think of him as a savior.

8. The Spiritually Curious are likely to DIY (do-it-yourself) their spiritual direction.

In our do-it-yourself culture, people are accustomed to using search engines to find answers to their questions. They don't necessarily need another person to be their expert guide. Instead, as curious people contemplate their desire to grow spiritually, they may look to themselves as a trustworthy source more than they look to any other relationship, including religious leaders, family members, or friends.

DIY Guidance

On a recent visit, my doctor entered the treatment room and asked, "So, what do you think you have?"

What a provocative opening question!

"I know you've googled all of your symptoms and have been reading. Tell me where you've landed."

My doctor understood that DIY culture means more than using YouTube tutorials for help unclogging a toilet, making a car repair, or learning to play the guitar. People are using the internet to care for themselves. The internet has become our owner's manual for life, and that includes things like our physical health and even our mental health and relationships. We'd be fooling ourselves to think people aren't doing this with spiritual pursuits and questions as well.

Now, I am not promoting a DIY faith where people can pick and choose their own beliefs. But we need to recognize that people are not as confident in traditional sources. Many of them feel like traditional sources have been a source of disappointment and even hurt. They don't want an intermediary expert between themselves and spiritual truth. They want to get rid of the middleman, diving in on their own and only turning to experts once they've grown comfortable with the landscape.

This is particularly true of Millennials, in large part because the experts and authorities have let them down in just about every field since they were teenagers. With crooked sports figures; lying government officials; business leaders who took care of themselves while their employees suffered; religious leaders who resigned because of greed, pride, or sexual misconduct; the "big short" that led to the 2008 market collapse then the cover-ups that followed; and the notion that nobody trusts media outlets anymore—people no longer have confidence in institutions and leaders the way they did in the past. Millennials are sometimes called the "unlucky generation," because between 9/11, COVID-19, student loan debt, numerous financial collapses, and stagnant wages even as the cost of living skyrockets, many of them feel like they've spent their life playing by the rules and have very little to show for it. There is a sense, among young people especially, that the only one you can count on is yourself. While clearly seen among younger generations, the totality of the population across generations has been impacted. And that has led to—and is an example of—a breakdown in community.

DIY is not about constructing a new faith but understanding that people need the autonomy and resources to make decisions they can believe in. They aren't looking for a leader to dutifully follow down the one right path, no questions asked. They're looking for someone to curate their exploration and help them process what they learn along the way.

And that is why we need to see ourselves as guides—museum docents—on their journey. They want to and need to have the experience themselves but aren't put off having a friend accompany them along the way.

In *Faith for Exiles*, David Kinnaman and I introduced a concept to describe changes that were necessary to disciple others in light of the digital revolution's cultural shifts. The rapid awareness of diverse perspectives has caused us to experience what we call "digital Babylon," a pluralization of worldviews that leads to a chaotic and hectic pace of life that has challenged our identities.[6] Before the digital revolution, most people had to deliberately seek out new worldviews. And if they did seek them out, they were able to investigate them slowly and thoughtfully. Today, however, we are being bombarded with hundreds of disparate worldviews every day, at all times. They are coming at us too fast for most of us to even notice them, let alone analyze them.

Since we are living in this digital Babylon, Kinnaman and I made a case for the need to disciple people differently than we had in the past. We argued that we need to form disciples with resilience instead of strength to build a faith that lasts.

As a former youth minister, I used to focus on building a strong faith in youth that would stand the test of time. But there are many strong things that are actually quite fragile. Something that is too rigid can be snapped in two. Once it breaks, it's not easily rebuilt. It's often broken forever.

Being resilient is different than being strong. Resilient things are able to bend without breaking. In fact, much like the tension that occurs in the act of lifting weights, the bending often makes them even stronger. If something resilient is seemingly wiped out, it can spring back to life like a forest after a fire. This type of resilience is a better quality to build in a disciple than simple strength. Resilient disciples can be challenged, pushed, and stretched without compromising their overall structure.

We recognize that there are Christians who believe the spiritual/supernatural exists. In fact, they are quite convinced of it. They are committed to attending church, praying, and reading Scripture. From the outside, their faith looks strong, but it is, in fact, a façade. If challenged, this faith could easily crumble.

In recent years, we have seen a phenomenon known as *deconstructing* wherein Christians—usually in their young adult years, but not always—are tearing down some of that supposedly "strong" but fragile faith. Forty-three percent of people with some kind of Christian background (and 30 percent of all adults in the U.S.) say they have "deconstructed the faith of their youth" (see Spiritually Open survey on p. 228).

It's caused quite a bit of concern. In later chapters, I'll explain why we need to see deconstructing as a positive. But for the time being, I want you to be open to the idea that this rapid shift brought on by digital Babylon has also resulted in an era of spiritual openness, and this era is revealing the fragility of our discipleship. *Faith for Exiles* came out just before the pandemic and was a bit prophetic, but I strongly believe that we haven't completely grasped the lesson that the pandemic offered.

COVID-19 gave the church an opportunity that we likely haven't fully leaned into. I conducted hundreds of hours of webinars during the pandemic, many with concerned church leaders wanting to know when we would get "back to normal." I implored leaders to take advantage of the moment. The institutional church has needed an update: the pandemic offered an opportunity to have a massive garage sale. Instead of "getting back to normal," I argued that this was a chance to create a much-needed new normal—one better equipped to meet the challenges of today.

I facilitated numerous workshops with church and nonprofit leaders, and one of the games we played was "keep it, curb it, refresh it." Never before has the church had an opportunity to "curb" so many relics we have accumulated over time. Enough with putting new wine into old wineskins.

Let's start thinking about what new things God is interested in doing through us.

What those workshops revealed to me was this: the Christian worldview has "hyper stagnated" with the rapid onset of digital Babylon. The world has changed at a breakneck pace, and much of the church's response was a reactionary position of defensiveness. The more digital Babylon shifts, the more the world shifts with it.

A Closer Look at the Spiritually Curious

THEY PRACTICE A SPIRITUALITY THAT IS . . .

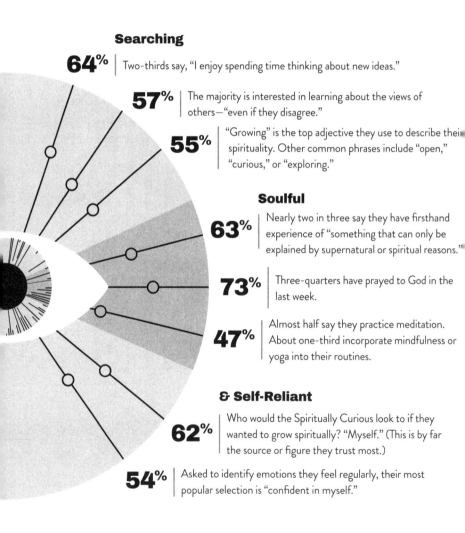

Searching

64% | Two-thirds say, "I enjoy spending time thinking about new ideas."

57% | The majority is interested in learning about the views of others—"even if they disagree."

55% | "Growing" is the top adjective they use to describe their spirituality. Other common phrases include "open," "curious," or "exploring."

Soulful

63% | Nearly two in three say they have firsthand experience of "something that can only be explained by supernatural or spiritual reasons."

73% | Three-quarters have prayed to God in the last week.

47% | Almost half say they practice meditation. About one-third incorporate mindfulness or yoga into their routines.

& Self-Reliant

62% | Who would the Spiritually Curious look to if they wanted to grow spiritually? "Myself." (This is by far the source or figure they trust most.)

54% | Asked to identify emotions they feel regularly, their most popular selection is "confident in myself."

n=200 U.S. adults who are Nonpracticing Christians or non-Christians, February 19–23, 2023. Source: Barna Group

It's useful to identify the beliefs of those outside the church who exhibit great spiritual openness. But we gain a more vibrant picture when we also examine their temperament, relationships, and routines. Here are some of their standout traits.

THEY EXHIBIT A CURIOSITY THAT MANIFESTS IN . . .

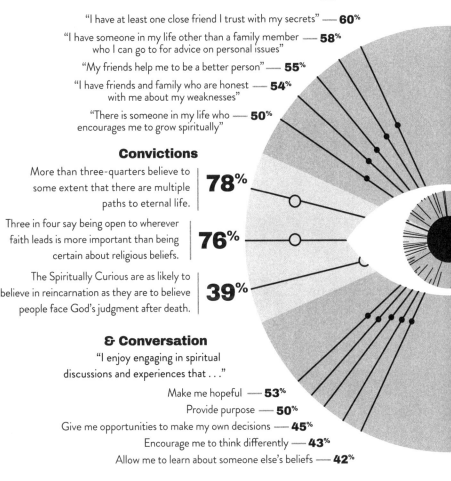

Community

Most spiritually curious people are in relationships that call them toward something greater.

"I have at least one close friend I trust with my secrets" — **60**%

"I have someone in my life other than a family member — **58**% who I can go to for advice on personal issues"

"My friends help me to be a better person" — **55**%

"I have friends and family who are honest — **54**% with me about my weaknesses"

"There is someone in my life who — **50**% encourages me to grow spiritually"

Convictions

More than three-quarters believe to some extent that there are multiple paths to eternal life. | **78**%

Three in four say being open to wherever faith leads is more important than being certain about religious beliefs. | **76**%

The Spiritually Curious are as likely to believe in reincarnation as they are to believe people face God's judgment after death. | **39**%

& Conversation

"I enjoy engaging in spiritual discussions and experiences that . . ."

Make me hopeful — **53**%
Provide purpose — **50**%
Give me opportunities to make my own decisions — **45**%
Encourage me to think differently — **43**%
Allow me to learn about someone else's beliefs — **42**%

3

The Curious Skeptic

One thing I love about doing research is that you always have work. No research project answers all the questions, and one project opens up questions for the next.

This is true as we try to understand the Spiritually Curious. We all bring assumptions to our research queries, and I originally thought of the curious as one large group. But in the process of doing statistical analysis, Barna's researchers and I discovered that among non-Christians and Nonpracticing Christians who were curious, there really were two categories of people: the Spiritually Curious and what we came to call the Curious Skeptics, who I briefly introduced before.

I wrestled with whether to keep them lumped into one group, but the differences were stark. The Spiritually Curious group—without the Curious Skeptics—was really who I wanted to write about. But the Curious Skeptics are a significant group, and it makes sense to spend a little time sharing the differences.

Characteristics of Curious Skeptics

Both groups score higher on our Curiosity Scale, but their respective worldviews about the supernatural is what makes them two distinct groups. The Spiritually Curious have strong convictions about the existence of a supernatural world. Curious Skeptics believe there is no way to know this (62 percent) or are unsure of their beliefs (38 percent). The Spiritually Curious are convinced that there is some sort of spiritual realm. The Curious Skeptics aren't as convinced but aren't closed to the possibility.

Because of this, you'll see many Curious Skeptics show some belief along the way, usually influenced by their personal experiences with the supernatural. These beliefs vary widely among the Curious Skeptics, so it's difficult to predict them with any consistency. That's why personal relationships are the best context for understanding these individuals, as opposed to relying entirely on the broad labels we use here.

There are some characteristics that we do find frequently in this group though.

Curious Skeptics Are Less Certain of Spiritual Concepts Than the Spiritually Curious

The distinguishing trait of the Spiritually Curious versus the Curious Skeptics is how certain these people are about a spiritual reality. Two-thirds of the Spiritually Curious (64 percent) are "completely certain" that there is a spiritual dimension to life, as opposed to just 20 percent of the Curious Skeptics. The Spiritually Curious are not necessarily confident that they understand the details of this spiritual dimension, but they are largely convinced of its existence. The Curious Skeptics are far less certain.

Similarly, we see that 54 percent of the Spiritually Curious are completely convinced that there is an afterlife, compared to just 22 percent of the Curious Skeptics. The Spiritually Curious are more likely to believe in heaven (50 percent) and hell (37 percent) than are the Curious Skeptics (24 percent and 13 percent, respectively). Moreover, a stunning 70 percent of the Spiritually Curious believe that there are things science can't explain, compared to just 43 percent of Curious Skeptics.

So as we can see, some Curious Skeptics aren't completely closed off to the idea of a supernatural realm. They just approach it from a position of skepticism.

Curious Skeptics Place Limits on Supernatural Possibilities

For each of the following, please indicate how certain you are:
% completely certain

	All U.S. adults	Practicing Christians	Spiritually Curious	Curious Skeptics	Naturalists
There are things that science cannot explain	56%	76%	70%	43%	27%
Heaven is a real place	44%	83%	50%	24%	1%
There is a spiritual dimension to life	42%	70%	64%	20%	–
There is an afterlife	40%	74%	54%	22%	–
Hell is a real place	32%	67%	37%	13%	3%

n=1,501 U.S. adults, February 19–23, 2023. Source: Barna Group

Curious Skeptics Have Interest in Spiritual Experiences and Want More of Them

What I really want to point out about the Curious Skeptic is that they are the easiest to mistake for a Naturalist. And when we, as Practicing Christians, talk to Curious Skeptics as if they are strict Naturalists, we tend to push them away.

As we have discussed, Naturalists make up a very small percentage of the overall population. What sets the Curious Skeptic apart is their lack of conviction about the supernatural world and the origin of the universe. Remember, the Naturalist believes there isn't anything beyond what can be experienced with the five senses and explained through the scientific method. The Curious Skeptic isn't so sure. Even if the skeptic doesn't believe we "can know" the answer, they are open to the idea that a higher power (likely God) created the universe.

It's important to note that only 19 percent of Curious Skeptics believe there is no such thing as God. One out of three believe in a Judeo-Christian concept of God. Nearly one out of six believe that God is the realization of human potential—that is, what humanity calls "God" is more of a collective consciousness, or something to that effect (see the chart on p. 158).

To understand the distinction I'm making here, and why we need to be careful about treating Curious Skeptics like Naturalists, let's dive a little deeper into the differences between these two groups.

Curious Skeptics Are More Willing Than Naturalists to Explore New Beliefs

While the Curious Skeptics are not as open as the Spiritually Curious, they welcome opportunities to explore new beliefs, once again showing the importance of thinking through the curious lens in our outreach efforts.

Curious Skeptics Are More Willing Than Naturalists to Be Open to Thinking Differently

While Naturalists are rather set in their ways and quite comfortable with being so, Curious Skeptics tell us they are open to spiritual discussions that encourage them to think differently. They see their beliefs as wet clay—still being formed and still subject to being molded and remolded by new experiences and information.

Curious Skeptics Are More Often Looking for Hope and Meaning in Spiritual Conversations

This is critical to keep in mind. While the Curious Skeptic may want to debate, they are looking for different outcomes to these debates than their Naturalist counterparts. The Curious Skeptic is looking for hope and meaning in their spiritual discussions even more than they're looking for certainty.

A World of Curiosity

People who haven't spent much time around Christians are often surprised to find how much diversity of thought is present in the church. There are Calvinists who believe God has predestined people to heaven, and there are Arminians who believe God has left that choice up to humans. There are Christians who baptize infants and Christians who baptize only adults. There are Christians who prefer the King James Version and Christians who prefer the New

International Version. Sometimes these various subgroups of Christians get along swimmingly. Sometimes things get a little testy. But the point is that one can't paint the whole segment of humanity who identify as Christian with one broad brush.

In the same way, we Christians need to be careful about painting those who are spiritually curious with a broad brush. As we've seen, interest in faith takes several different forms. We need to take the time to understand the spiritually curious people we come across and get to know the particulars of their curiosity. Once we've recognized how many different ways there are to explore spirituality, we can start to answer their questions with the seriousness and enthusiasm that this inquisitiveness deserves.

The Miraculous

I recently had lunch with a self-identified atheist who I've known for nearly a decade. I believe if I shared the various categories I've developed for this project, he'd likely select the Curious Skeptic label for himself. He appreciated that I didn't always make our meetings have a spiritual focus, but he'd just returned from a trip to Israel, and I asked him what he found most meaningful.

While he wouldn't describe himself as having a spiritual experience, he did say the trip had made a profound impact on him, particularly poking some holes in the belief system he had constructed around his perspective on the spiritual aspects of life. This young man is incredibly intelligent and reflective; I could sense he was going through a moment of meaning-making. I offered to help.

Some of his struggle with belief was around many religious people's reliance on sacred texts. But after he visited the country where many of the events in these texts took place, he began to consider the credibility of the Scriptures as being more than pure fiction. He still struggled with miraculous incidents, like the parting of the Red Sea, but he theorized that some of these may have been perfectly natural incidents that grew exaggerated over time.

I believe in miracles, yet am more interested in the truths they teach. I shared how a popular biblical commentator, William Barclay, didn't believe in the supernatural nature of Jesus's miracles. Even though I read Barclay deeply in high school, I'd never realized he didn't believe in Jesus's literal miracles until I was in college, because the truths he pulled from them were life-changing.

I told my friend how the story of feeding the multitudes could have profound meaning whether a miracle literally occurred or not. It wasn't the miracle that truly mattered as much as what changed in people's hearts. Barclay doesn't believe Jesus literally multiplied food until there was enough for everyone, but the lesson he pulls out of it for our own lives is still valuable for us today:

> The people were hungry—and they were utterly selfish. They all had something with them, but they would not produce it for themselves in case they had to share it with others. The Twelve laid before the multitude their little store and thereupon others were moved to produce theirs; and in the end there was more than enough for everyone. So it may be regarded as a miracle which turned selfish, suspicious folk into generous people, a miracle of Christ's changing determined self-interest into a willingness to share.[1]

It was a brief conversation, but it ended with a more hopeful outlook and a new way to begin to embrace the truth of Scripture.

Now I must tell you, when I—at the super-wise age of twenty—learned that Barclay didn't embrace the miracles of Jesus, I didn't read any more of his commentaries for at least a decade. I was so disillusioned. And yet, here I was years later, using the example of Barclay to help a Curious Skeptic begin to trust that the text of Scripture is alive and capable of helping him know Jesus in a way he never imagined.

To journey with a Curious Skeptic is one of the greatest joys we can have as a believer. This unique type of skeptic can often help us deepen our own faith, because we find we have to trust Jesus as we help them do the same.

The Afterlife

At some point on the journey with a Curious Skeptic, there will come a time when the subject of the afterlife enters the discussion (and my experience is most people are open to sharing their views on this topic). This is another opportunity to offer hope. The research shows that more than half (58 percent) of Curious Skeptics don't know what will happen to them when they die (see the chart on p. 129). This can be great to explore in conversation. Although an overwhelming majority of Naturalists feel similarly, that group is significantly more likely than any other to believe we simply cease to exist, whereas the Spiritually Curious believe equally in reincarnation and judgment before God.

Interestingly, a large number of U.S. adults ascribe to the traditional Judeo-Christian view that they will face some

How Curiosity Intersects with Views of the Afterlife

Which of the following comes closest to describing your view about what happens when a person dies?

	All U.S. adults	Practicing Christians	Spiritually Curious	Curious Skeptics	Naturalists
They face judgment before God for their decisions here on earth	45%	72%	39%	36%	4%
Their spirit is reincarnated and comes back to earth in another form	21%	16%	39%	17%	7%
Their spirit is terminated and ceases to exist	17%	4%	5%	25%	58%
Something else	17%	8%	16%	21%	32%

n=1,501 U.S. adults, February 19–23, 2023. Source: Barna Group

kind of judgment for the life they have lived. Even in our postmodern, post-Christian culture, 45 percent believe they will be judged for their moral choices when their life comes to an end. Perhaps there is something here that can give us insight into how we might reach people for Christ.

A Sermon for Pagans

While it seems we've been talking about post-Christian culture in the United States for only a couple of decades, intellectuals like C. S. Lewis have been using the term since the 1940s to describe postwar Europe. In the 1946 Christmas issue of *The Strand* magazine, Lewis published "A Christmas

Sermon for Pagans," where he addressed the realities of post-Christianity in European culture. There may be no author or intellectual who has had more appeal or success in converting skeptics than Lewis (after all, he was just such a skeptic himself before turning to Jesus), and his wisdom in this little-known "sermon" gives us some insight into how we might address skeptics in an age of spiritual openness. I'm going to excerpt it at some length here.

When I was asked to write a Christmas sermon for Pagans I accepted the job lightheartedly enough: but now that I sit down to tackle it I discover a difficulty. Are there any Pagans in England for me to write to?

I know that people keep on telling us that this country is relapsing into Paganism. But they only mean it is ceasing to be Christian. And is that at all the same thing? Let us remember what a Pagan or Heathen (I use the words interchangeably) really was.

A "Heathen" meant a man who lived out on the heath, out in the wilds. A "Pagan" meant a man who lived in a Pagus or small village. Both words, in fact, meant a "rustic" or "yokel." They date from the time when the larger towns of the Roman Empire were already Christianised, but the old Nature religions still lingered in the country. Pagans or Heathens were the backward people in the remote districts who had not yet been converted, who were still pre-Christian.

To say that modern people who have drifted away from Christianity are Pagans is to suggest that a post-Christian man is the same as a pre-Christian man. And that is like thinking that a woman who has lost her husband is the same sort of person as an unmarried girl: or that a street where the houses have been knocked down is the same as a field where no house has yet been built.[2]

This is a valuable insight: the notion that the "post-Christian" is not the same as a "pre-Christian." Lewis goes on to list three ways the pagan differed from the post-Christian person.

Now the real Pagan differed from the post-Christian in the following ways.

Firstly, he was religious. From the Christian point of view he was indeed too religious by half. He was full of reverence. To him the earth was holy, the woods and waters were alive. His agriculture was a ritual as well as a technique. And secondly, he believed in what we now call an "Objective" Right or Wrong. That is, he thought the distinction between pious and impious acts was something which existed independently of human opinions: something like the multiplication table which Man had not invented but had found to be true and which (like the multiplication table) he had better take notice of. The gods would punish him if he did not.

To be sure, by Christian standards, his list of "Right" or "Wrong" acts was rather a muddled one. He thought (and the Christians agreed) that the gods would punish him for setting the dogs on a beggar who came to his door or for striking his father: but he also thought they would punish him for turning his face to the wrong point of the compass when he began ploughing. But though his code included some fantastic sins and duties, it got in most of the real ones.

And this leads us to the third great difference between a Pagan and a post-Christian man. Believing in a real Right and Wrong means finding out that you are not very good.

It occurred to him that he himself might be one of the things that was wrong with the world. He knew he had sinned. And the terrible thing was that he thought the gods made no difference between voluntary and involuntary sins.[3]

Lewis's insight into the challenges of reaching the Curious Skeptic hinges greatly on our ability to understand that the journey to Christ for the post-Christian requires an extra set of steps. In fact, Lewis concludes the sermon with this:

> If the modern post-Christian view is wrong—and every day I find it harder to think it right—then there are three kinds of people in the world. (1) Those who are sick and don't know it (the post-Christians). (2) Those who are sick and know it (Pagans). (3) Those who have found the cure. And if you start in the first class you must go through the second to reach the third. For (in a sense) all that Christianity adds to Paganism is the cure.[4]

In 1947, Lewis explored the challenges of reaching those who he believed to be in a spiritually worse state than they would have been before Christianity existed for them. He delved into this topic through a series of so-called Latin Letters exchanged with the Italian priest Don Giovanni Calabria. Despite the language barrier, their correspondence transcended linguistic limitations. For a period of seven years, Lewis and Calabria engaged in a heartfelt exchange, until Calabria's passing in 1954.

An excerpt from those letters gives us insight into how we might approach the Curious Skeptic of our age.

For my part, I believe we ought to work not only at spreading the Gospel (that certainly) but also to a certain preparation for the Gospel. It is necessary to recall many to the law of nature before we talk about God. For Christ promises forgiveness of sins, but what is that to those who, since they do not know the law of nature, do not know that they have sinned? Who will take medicine unless he knows he is in the grip of a disease? Moral relativity is the enemy we have to overcome before we tackle atheism. I would almost dare to say, "First let us make the younger generation good pagans, and afterwards let us make them Christians."[5]

Lewis's last line—"let us make them good pagans, and then Christians" (to paraphrase)—summarizes some of the work to be done with the Curious Skeptic.

Helping the Curious Skeptic

Conversations with Curious Skeptics are interesting, enriching situations for everyone involved. In my experience, there are a few paths forward to help them effectively explore some of their questions with you.

Help Them Define Their Sense of Morality

One young skeptic told me he didn't need Christianity, as he had formed his own morality that was free of any sense of organized religion. I asked him to write down his moral code, which he did. Unsurprisingly, the list looked very much like the Ten Commandments—only slightly updated to specifically address some recent cultural immorality with greater specificity.

This particular person was surprised when I read the actual Ten Commandments to him and he saw the striking similarity. "What do you suppose may have informed your list?" I asked. I went on to ask if any one of his moral principles was "greater" than the others.

I then went on to explain a little about how Old Testament law worked, and I shared some of the Sermon on the Mount and how Jesus responded when asked to identify the greatest commandment.

Help Them Articulate Moral Responsibility in Life and Death

The research indicates there is a sense of accountability and judgment among all Curious types. Helping them recognize this reality will assist them with understanding the need for salvation that can come only from Jesus Christ.

When I talk to a Curious Skeptic, it's interesting to ask them about their understanding of right and wrong and find out what "doing good" and "doing bad" means for them. After looking at their list of moral statements, I ask them what the consequences might be for breaking any of those commitments.

I don't think I've had a person in recent years not express some standard of accountability that should be enforced. You could even say that the current phenomenon of cancel culture—holding public figures accountable via social pressure—reveals a kind of pagan-like accountability. But in this post-Christian world it becomes a bit muddy, and most people recognize the limitations of internet dogpiles as a substitute for true justice.

Ask Them If They Feel Accountable for How They Live according to This Moral Code

When I talk with Curious Skeptics, I often share the story of the rich young ruler. It's a great conversation "deepener" that can lead into a discussion of works versus grace. Our research indicates that less than 15 percent agree strongly that their good works are enough (see the chart on p. 129).

Having someone analyze how their life compares to their moral code takes the conversation from the theoretical to the personal. Do they have any moral accountability for their actions and, if so, to whom? Is this making any difference in the choices they make and, if not, why not?

As Lewis points out, those with a "pagan" worldview feel some moral responsibility for their actions; Curious Skeptics likely have never shared that with anyone but have probably thought about it to some extent, and this may impact their beliefs regarding what happens after death.

I've introduced two emerging worldviews in this age of spiritual openness: the Spiritually Curious and Curious Skeptic. Let's take a moment to look at Practicing Christians now in light of our exploration of the Spiritually Curious.

A Curious Culture

Practicing Christians, as we discussed earlier, are people who self-identify as Christians, have made a commitment to Jesus that is still important in their life today, and attend church at least monthly. The hypothesis that led to this research and, ultimately, this book was the idea that Practicing Christians differ from the Spiritually Curious in substantial enough ways that we might be unknowingly preventing the gospel from reaching the curious. That is, Practicing Christians might be trying to reach the Spiritually Curious in ways that the Spiritually Curious don't find compelling or interesting. Practicing Christians are trying to connect in ways that they themselves might find engaging, but the Spiritually Curious are looking for a different kind of engagement.

Knowing more about what this means and why this is happening is important for us as Practicing Christians. Whether you're a pastor, a leader in your church, or just someone who cares about the future of Christianity in your community, you owe it to yourself to understand this challenge and how you can rise to meet it.

It's important to note that Practicing Christians are very different than their Spiritually Curious counterparts in some significant ways. Look at the chart on page 77 to compare the two groups' responses to the items that make up our Curiosity Scale. While Practicing Christians don't entirely shy away from new information or opportunities to grow, they are less likely than the Spiritually Curious to agree on some level that they welcome challenges or embrace the unfamiliar or uncertain. You can see that, meanwhile, the Spiritually Curious have near-total enthusiasm for the new, complex, or unpredictable, they rarely disagree with any of the statements provided and see many scenarios as a chance to learn and grow.

Take a moment and imagine you are designing and marketing one product for Practicing Christians and another for the Spiritually Curious. In what ways would they be different? How would each group's preferences differ?

In the realm of anthropology, *culture* is a term that carries profound significance. It's a concept that transcends the surface-level phenomena we often associate with it like music, art, cuisine, and attire. Culture is something deeper and more difficult to articulate than just popular TV shows and trendy fashions. So what exactly is culture?

Culture is the invisible thread that binds a group of people together. It's the shared patterns of behaviors, stories, values, tools, and understanding that are learned through a process of socialization. These patterns, which can be symbolic, linguistic, material, and behavioral, help individuals navigate their world and make sense of their experiences.

Practicing Christians Struggle to Welcome Newness or Uncertainty

Read each of the following statements and decide how much you agree with each according to your beliefs and experiences.

% agree (strongly, moderately, or slightly)

● Practicing Christians   ● Spiritually Curious

I like to do things that are a little frightening	46% 86%
I am the type of person who really enjoys the uncertainty of everyday life	50% 87%
I prefer jobs that are excitingly unpredictable	56% 92%
I am the kind of person who embraces unfamiliar people, events, and places	67% 98%
I am always looking for experiences that challenge how I think about myself and the world	75% 98%
I am at my best when doing something that is complex or challenging	77% 96%
Everywhere I go, I am out looking for new things or experiences	78% 99%
I frequently seek out opportunities to challenge myself and grow as a person	81% 97%
I view challenging situations as an opportunity to grow and learn	88% 97%
I actively seek as much information as I can in new situations	91% 99%

n=1,500 U.S. adults, February 19–23, 2023. Source: Barna Group

To put it in simpler terms, imagine you're dropped into an unfamiliar city without a map. You'd feel lost, right? What you need is a map that will help you understand where you are in this strange city and help you navigate where to go from there. Culture is a sort of societal map. It shapes our values, beliefs, and norms, influencing how we think, behave, react, and communicate. If you don't understand a particular community's culture, you're just as lost as you would be in a strange city with no map.

Moreover, culture is not static; it evolves over time, responding to changes in the environment, technological advancements, and interaction with other cultures and groups of people. It's the dynamic tapestry of human life, woven from countless threads of shared experiences, traditions, and knowledge.

So when we talk about culture, we're talking about the fundamental blueprint that guides people, the collective programming of the mind that distinguishes the members of one cultural group from another. It's an intangible concept, but it has an impact on nearly every facet of our lives.

Over a period of about ten years, I've been involved in helping merge several different organizations. I've also helped launch new organizations out of existing ones. While all had similar ministry objectives and business realities, that didn't mean the way they did things was similar. Each organization had a unique culture and set of systems used within it, and that meant each required unique processes and adaptions to ensure buy-in and a successful merger or launch.

I learned in my college intercultural studies course how to combat my ingrained assumptions and ways of thinking, speaking, and behaving to interact well with people from very different places; onboarding into a new organization can require those same skills. This is because institutional cultures can be deep-seated without our even being aware of how they developed, how jarring our way of doing things is to someone from the outside, and how much our identity is now wrapped up in extraneous things.

Let's dive into this further by using a long-running technology debate. Consider for a moment what an organization's IT preferences tell us about its culture. One organization might use Windows computers. Another uses Macs. Both machines do the same basic functions but are seen as radically different (to the point that many have very strong allegiances to one versus the other and feel deep attachments to their chosen brand ecosystem). Often, the operating system chosen by an organization reveals something about its cultural values and identity, even if its members can't tell you why they originally chose one over the other. Following the stereotypes, one ministry places a higher value on aesthetics while another cares more about saving money. Both can be fiscally responsible, but their offices (and what they wear to work!) are likely quite different. Neither choice is right or wrong. But those choices tell us a good deal about what kind of culture we're working with, and this can excite some prospective employees while repelling others.

The Bible records some major cultural clashes. In the book of Daniel, we see two cultures coming together: Babylon and Israel. We learn how Daniel and some of the other young men taken into service in Nebuchadnezzar's palace navigated these conflicts, balancing what was important to their identities with learning to live and work in the culture of Babylon.

I want to begin making the point here, through these examples, that we Practicing Christians have likely developed a "cognitive culture" that simply does not appeal, or make sense, to a spiritually curious person. If we want to reach the Spiritually Curious, we will have to evolve our own cognitive church cultures to be a place where they can tell they have a seat at the table.

Data, analysis, and introspection can be valuable to us as we think about how we create ministry. We are either intentional in the culture we create, or it just happens: but it *will* happen. Data can help us see our worldview in comparison to others and help us make choices that take varying perspectives and backgrounds into consideration.

We will explore this more fully later in this chapter. But first, it might be instructive to ask why Practicing Christians have a markedly different take on curiosity than the Spiritually Curious? If culture is learned and shared, where might our less-than-curious culture come from?

Where to Find What You Need to Know

When my great-grandmother passed away, she left my family a little bit of money. One night my parents unveiled what we were going to purchase. My brothers and I imagined a new television with one of those new VCRs or maybe a vacation to Disneyland. Drumroll, please. My parents gathered us around the table and announced we were going to be getting a set of encyclopedias!

While we have a great deal of books in our home, my kids would probably laugh if I thought that was a worthwhile investment in today's age of information. But at the time, that encyclopedia set leveled up my reputation in some big ways. Friends would call the night before a project was due to see if they could come by and use them because the library was closed. It was fun to pull them off the shelf when a particular topic came up and even just to peruse them from time to time looking for interesting information. It was like a small, tangible version of Google.

I learned a lot from those encyclopedias, but the most important lesson came the day we unpacked them. My dad held up a volume and said, "Mark, you can spend a lifetime going to school, but you'll never learn everything. The most important thing you can learn is where to find what you need to know."

My dad's wisdom has stuck with me, particularly in the internet age. As I became older, and particularly with the explosion of digital connectivity, an important assumption I've always had is that if I thought of something, someone else probably already had thought of it, and they were likely smarter than me. So I should go find them. Chances are, they're a good resource to find what you need to know.

When I first wondered about curiosity, I stumbled on a book called *A Curious Mind* by movie producer Brian Grazer. It detailed his lifelong pursuit of curiosity and his practice of obtaining interviews with great minds from all backgrounds. A favorite story from his life was when he secured an interview with the great science fiction author Isaac Asimov. Ten minutes into the interview, Asimov's wife shut it down because it was clear to her that Grazer didn't know enough about Asimov to warrant continuing the interview![1] If her husband was going to give his time, the interviewer needed to value it enough to be prepared. An important lesson, to be sure.

As I set out to understand the Spiritually Curious, I wondered what the attitude toward curiosity had been in the church throughout time. How had Christian leaders treated the Spiritually Curious in the first century and during the Middle Ages? Had the curious been welcomed or treated with suspicion?

It's an important question. After all, cautionary tales of being too curious permeate Western culture. In addition to the classic proverb "Curiosity killed the cat," we have tales of Pandora's Box, Goldilocks, Jack and the Beanstalk, and Icarus, all of which caution us against being too curious. In the biblical text, Eve's curiosity unleashes knowledge of good and evil that leads to death, and Lot's wife turns around to look at Sodom and Gomorrah and turns into a pillar of salt. It's not hard to see how some Christians could interpret those stories as a warning against curiosity.

These stories seem to suggest that curiosity is less virtue and more vice. So how did early Christians think about curiosity?

I put the lesson learned while unpacking those encyclopedias with my father to the test, and I found there are smarter people than me who have done deeper work than I am likely to ever be able to do. Not only have they answered the questions I was seeking, they've done it with excellence. Neil Kenny wrote *The Uses of Curiosity in Early Modern France and Germany*, which led me to Joseph Torchia's book *Restless Mind Curiositas & the Scope of Inquiry in St. Augustine's Psychology*. Both books are fascinating to read if you have time.

In our modern world, curiosity is often celebrated as a virtue. It is seen as the driving force behind innovation, discovery, and learning. We praise curiosity in children and generally encourage it in our schools. But in early Europe, curiosity was a major source of contentious discussion in universities, churches, newspapers, and other purveyors of contemporary thought. Kenny's book explores just how widespread the discussion was, from how to define curiosity to how it should be regulated among the populace.

You and I may not be aware of the fine details of these past debates, but we are nevertheless shaped by them today. These conversations are part of our legacy and helped form our current attitudes about curiosity. With that in mind, maybe we should take a moment to reflect on how our attitudes may be a product of the generations of culture shapers before us. And when it comes to people who shaped the culture of Christianity, few names loom larger than Augustine of Hippo.

Saint Augustine had a nuanced perspective of curiosity. He recognized its potential benefits but also warned of its dangers. His moral triad consisted of three vices: pride, curiosity, and carnal concupiscence. In his framework, pride was a lust for domination while concupiscence was lust of the flesh, and Christians ought to avoid both. In the same way, Augustine saw curiosity as an unrestricted lust for knowledge—a passion to know things just for the sake of knowing them. Augustine taught that each of these vices prompted the soul's movement toward some aspect of unhealthy worldly experience.

My reading of these two academic volumes led me to imagine Augustine writing an internet blog post called "Three Warnings regarding Curiosity." Since he isn't here to write it, I'll summarize what I think would have been his focus.

Curiosity as a Transgression

Augustine saw curiosity as a component of his moral triad, and he associated it with the audacity to disobey the divine command, the set of moral imperatives and teachings that come from God, which are meant to guide human behavior toward the good and away from sin. He viewed curiosity as a sort of lust of the mind, a voracious need to know that could never be satiated. This curiosity, according to Augustine, came coupled with an eagerness to experience what is unknown. He believed that curiosity could lead to transgressions and a desire to experience anything and everything—up to and including sinful things forbidden by God.

When Eve transgressed against God by eating the forbidden fruit, she had no idea or imagination of what evil was. She may have been warned that eating the fruit would lead to death, but Scripture doesn't give us any indication she understood what death was. Curiosity, as they say, got the better of her.

While we have a much more seasoned experience with sin than Eve did, we too can find ourselves in a situation where we do not understand God's laws fully. We may understand that we are going against God's command, but we don't fully grasp the stakes in play. Our mind cannot imagine how we might be injured or why our relationship with God might suffer through our transgression. And curiosity to know just what we're missing out on can lead us to cross the boundaries.

Curiosity as an Impediment to Truth

Augustine also saw curiosity as a potential impediment to our ability to discern truth. He associated curiosity with the "lust of the eyes," linking the human craving for knowledge with the love of worldly experience. He didn't think it was healthy for people to want to know too much about the world, since it could lead to us relying on our own understanding instead of godly revelation. This warning is particularly relevant in our current age of information overload, where the pursuit of knowledge can often lead us away from truth and into the realm of misinformation and superficial understanding.

This danger can be very subtle. Sometimes, it can even look like discipleship. We explore the truths of God's Word so deeply we lose sight of the main thing, getting so caught up in small details of the faith that the work of actually following Jesus falls by the wayside. This has been true of God's people throughout Scripture and history. In our desire to know all that we can, we sin. Some religious leaders in Jesus's day had written pages upon pages about how to apply purity to living holy lives in their own contemporary conditions but failed to commune with God and others in loving sacrifice. Paul warns the church in Corinth that even if all knowledge and mysteries are understood, we can still miss what is important. Indeed, knowledge can "puff" us up, even if that knowledge is true.

Curiosity as a Moral Hazard

In his pastoral work, Augustine counseled against unrestricted curiosity. He saw it as a morally hazardous realm. He saw the *curiositas* of pagans as the *curiositas* of every person who inhabits the earthly city, exerting a powerful influence. This warning reminds us that curiosity, when not tempered by wisdom and discernment, can lead us down harmful and destructive paths.

Augustine wasn't off base here. It's true that curiosity can lead us into moral failure. I remember when my daughter and I went out to dinner one night when she was in sixth grade (most people would call these daddy-daughter dates, but she thought that sounded creepy, so we just had dinner).

She wanted to try frog legs, so we went to a nearby restaurant that had them on the menu. As we were waiting for our food, my daughter asked me if I'd ever tried drugs.

Just to be clear, she wasn't offering them to me. She just wanted to know if I'd ever done them. I told her that I had not.

Then she asked me another question, "Would you try them if they were legal?"

At the time, marijuana had been legalized in Colorado and Washington, so the issue was coming up quite a bit in everyday discussion.

Well, now she had me in an interesting theoretical position. I'd never really thought about drug use because it had always been illegal. I'd also grown up in the thick of Nancy Reagan's "Just Say No" crusade. The "This Is Your Brain on Drugs" public service commercials from the 1980s depicted the harmful effects of drug use by showing a fried egg sizzling in a pan. As far as my own personal experience went, the campaign was a huge success. These images were etched in my mind. But I realized my daughter was growing up in a very different world than I did, with fewer stigmas and laws around smoking weed.

I looked into my daughter's eyes and said, "You know, you and I are a lot alike. We are curious people. We want to experience everything in life, whether good or bad, just for the experience. I haven't done drugs, primarily because they are illegal. But I know if they were legal, my curiosity would tempt me to at least want to try it once. And that is why people like you and I have to be careful, Skye. We can't let our curiosity lead us down a potentially dangerous path."

Maybe Augustine was onto something with his warnings about *curiositas*.

On the other hand, it was Augustine's curiosity about the spiritual world that would shape how many of us understand, think about, and practice our Christian faith. Books like *Confessions* and *City of God* are among the most influential books on Christian faith of all time. Those books wouldn't be very interesting if Augustine wasn't at least a little curious about the Christian faith.

While curiosity can be a mark of a vigorous intellect and a driver of intellectual striving, Augustine's warnings remind us of the need for discernment, wisdom, and a commitment to truth in our pursuit of knowledge. As we navigate our modern world, filled with endless opportunities for learning and discovery, let us heed Augustine's warnings and strive to cultivate a curiosity that leads us closer to truth, wisdom, and ultimately, to God.

Augustine's framing helps us understand why we may have developed a less-than-curious culture in our church practices over time and why the church's age-old suspicion of curiosity may have some grounding in real concern. But if we want to reach the curious, we may need to realize how far the church is from what they may be looking to experience. We may even have some Spiritually Curious in our midst who are struggling in our high-certainty culture. Rarely has there been a better time to address these challenges.

A Culture of Certainty

In middle school, I convinced my mother to buy me a small poster I found while visiting a Christian bookstore. It was simple, chunky black text overlaid on a nauseating Pepto Bismol–pink background. The poster is still in my bedroom at my parents' house, and I still taste the Pepto pink when I see it. I overlooked the fact that it didn't fit my style because I found the words on it so compelling: "God said it! I believe it! That settles it!"

As a teenager, I was keen on public speaking (I was class president from middle school through my senior year of high school and sat as the student representative on the school board for our district). I enjoyed communicating my opinions and beliefs and was confident in my convictions. To say I was quick to speak and slow to think would be an understatement. The truth is, I'm still haunted by some of the things I said in those days—the times my confidence tipped over into arrogance.

I was also bold regarding my faith. My identity was formed during President Reagan's tenure, which was accompanied by the rise of the Moral Majority. While this era cultivated a love for civil engagement among many firm, passionate believers, it was often accompanied by a troubling cocktail of faith and patriotism. As a young man, I wasn't always able to distinguish between my identity as a Christian and my identity as an American. Today we would call this Christian Nationalism, and while I now regret buying into it, it made older Christians quite proud of me at the time. In fact, it was the attention of adults in my church and community that shaped me; they loved to see a young person act with such boldness. I must confess, this unwavering confidence in my interpretation of Scripture fueled my fearlessness in engaging in debates and challenging those who held differing viewpoints—often with very little consideration for how I was coming across. In my mind, it was my evangelical duty to confront those with alternative perspectives, because I was convinced that my fervent opposition would serve as an undeniable pathway to their salvation. Paul told the Ephesians to speak the truth in love. I was doing a pretty good job of speaking the truth, as I understood it at the time. But the "in love" part was a struggle.

I now cringe at the lack of intellectual humility I possessed as a young Christian, and my obsession with being right over being in a right relationship with Jesus. I was more interested in telling my friends they were wrong than finding out whether they actually followed Jesus.

I was a teenage Pharisee.

I had grown up at the church I attended. In fact, my parents did too. Their parents—my grandparents—helped plant the church as laypeople. When I say they built the church, I'm not just speaking figuratively. I have pictures of my grandfather riding the tops of the beams of the sanctuary as the building was under construction. Everyone I grew up with was part of a multi-gen churchgoing family.

And then I met Jay. Our youth pastors were really good—almost too good—at reaching out to unchurched kids in our neighborhood. Jay came from a nearby apartment complex, and when he visited the church and began following Jesus, his faith took off. His spiritual appetite was off the charts. He was soaring. Meanwhile, I was in coast mode, believing I had pretty much mastered this Christian life thing.

And yet, I marveled at Jay's hunger for the Lord and the radical way he set out to follow Jesus every day of his life. It actually made me quite jealous, much like the brother who stayed home in the parable of the prodigal son. Seeing Jay's intense curiosity to learn more about God sparked something in me. It pushed me to rethink just how much I really had Christianity down.

It wasn't until the end of my senior year that I really came to know and understand the person of Jesus and what it meant to follow him. There was so much more to it than just being right, letting everyone else know how right I was, and never entertaining the possibility that I still had more to learn and—who knows?—maybe even some things to unlearn. My high need for closure had actually been a barrier to my ability to follow Jesus well. Even worse, it had been a barrier to my ability to share the Good News with others. No one wants to listen to a guy who is always talking and never listening, always teaching and never learning.

It turns out I'm not the only one striving to bring closure to spiritual interactions and conversations.

The Need for Closure

In 1994, D. M. Webster and A. W. Kruglanski developed and published the Need for Closure Scale (NFCS) to gauge an individual's inclination toward seeking definitive answers and their discomfort with ambiguity.[2] Essentially, using a list of fifteen items, it measures how at ease we are with uncertainty.

The research Barna conducted for this project looked at not only curiosity but also our need for closure, for certainty. Remember, a need for closure refers to a person's preference for structure, predictability, and certainty versus their interest in tension, questions, and exploration. Those with a high need for closure are more inclined to make a decision with a lower amount of information, whereas those with a lower need for closure are more comfortable taking their time to collect more data before making a call.

We found that Practicing Christians are more likely than those outside the church to have a high need for closure. Thirty-nine percent of Practicing Christians (two of five) have a high need for closure, versus 29 percent of Nonpracticing Christians and 27 percent of non-Christians.

To get a clearer idea of what a "high need for closure" might look like, take a look at some of Barna's findings in the

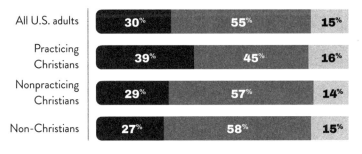

The Need for Closure Scale

Based on a 15-item metric, Practicing Christians are more likely than other faith groups to have a high need for closure or certainty.

● High need for closure   ● Moderate need for closure   ● Low need for closure

	High need for closure	Moderate need for closure	Low need for closure
All U.S. adults	30%	55%	15%
Practicing Christians	39%	45%	16%
Nonpracticing Christians	29%	57%	14%
Non-Christians	27%	58%	15%

n=1,501 U.S. adults, February 19–23, 2023. Source: Barna Group fascinating chart on page 93. In every instance, you'll see that Practicing Christians are more likely than Nonpracticing Christians and non-Christians to express discomfort with tension, uncertainty, and mystery.

It was intriguing to discover that Practicing Christians generally exhibit a higher need for closure compared to non-Christians. This disparity may stem from the Christian faith's emphasis on clear-cut beliefs. Practicing Christians' propensity for closure also seems to come from a desire for comfort. Some of the survey items that most inspire their agreement are "I enjoy having a clear and structured mode of life" and "When I have made a decision, I feel relieved." Other faith groups are far less enthusiastic about having these experiences. Regardless of the underlying reasons, Practicing Christians' bent toward consistency and closure offers a fascinating insight into the intersection of religion and personality.

I am not suggesting that all Christians possess a high need for closure. Nor am I suggesting that having a high need for closure is a bad thing, in and of itself. Our research shows that it's more complex than that. However, it does raise an important question: If we, as believers, do in fact have a higher need for closure or serve congregants who do, how might this be affecting the culture we are fostering in our churches?

We can at least assume that those *outside* our churches will struggle to relate to and connect with us. Many Nonpracticing Christians and non-Christians don't just have a low need for closure—they hold respect for openness. They even seem to find enjoyment in it! Consider that, when asked to describe their spiritual beliefs today, people of no faith

Practicing Christians Prefer Comfort, Closure & Clarity

Read each of the following statements and decide how much you agree with each according to your beliefs and experiences.

% strongly agree

	All U.S. adults	Practicing Christians	Nonpracticing Christians	Non-Christians
When I have made a decision, I feel relieved	30%	41%	28%	28%
I enjoy having a clear and structured mode of life	28%	43%	26%	25%
I find that establishing a consistent routine enables me to enjoy life more	26%	33%	27%	22%
I don't like to go into a situation without knowing what I can expect from it	24%	30%	22%	23%
I find that a well-ordered life with regular hours suits my temperament	22%	29%	21%	19%
I dislike unpredictable situations	21%	23%	18%	22%
I don't like situations that are uncertain	20%	25%	18%	19%
When I am confronted with a problem, I'm anxious to reach a solution very quickly	20%	22%	19%	21%
I don't like to be with people who are capable of unexpected actions	18%	25%	16%	16%
I feel uncomfortable when I don't understand the reason why an event occurred in my life	16%	20%	13%	17%
I dislike it when a person's statement could mean many different things	15%	18%	13%	15%
I dislike questions that could be answered in many different ways	11%	17%	12%	8%
I do not usually consult many different opinions before forming my own view	11%	14%	11%	11%
I would quickly become impatient and irritated if I would not find a solution to a problem immediately	10%	13%	9%	9%
I feel irritated when one person disagrees with what everyone else in a group believes	7%	13%	5%	6%

n=1,501 U.S. adults, February 19–23, 2023. Source: Barna Group tend to say, "I feel content that I don't have all the answers." While Practicing Christians are split on whether it matters more to them to "be certain in their religious beliefs" or to "be open to wherever their faith leads them," people of no faith overwhelmingly favor the latter. We see this in Nones' relationship to doubt as well. They welcome it, going so far as to say it is "good to be skeptical or doubting." By comparison, Christians see doubt as a challenge to be overcome. At most, they may concede it is "part of life's journey," but not the end goal.[3]

You can see how these differences may make it difficult for people of different faith persuasions to accompany each other on said journey. One party might be along for the ride (and all its detours) while the other is committed to diligently follow a map (and they brought their own snacks).

While certainty may provide comfort and a sense of security, it can also limit our growth and prevent us from asking good questions or learning new things. It's important to balance confidence with humility and to stay open to the new ideas and perspectives that God wants to teach us.

Curiosity versus Certainty: What's Your Comfort Level?

If you lean toward a need for closure, take a moment to consider how your church's preaching, teaching, and ministry programs might land with a person who has a lower need for certainty and a propensity for curiosity. Put yourself in the shoes of a person who is interested in exploring new ideas.

Remember, the Spiritually Curious want more of a museum tour guide than an answer key for a pop quiz.

1. Do your sermons provide clear-cut answers that remove any opportunity to engage, or do they help guide congregants to make their own discoveries?

   The purpose of content in today's world should be to unlock the doors to curiosity and inquiry. We need to create content that stimulates the mind and opens up new avenues for people to explore. A good teacher isn't just getting the class to memorize the correct answers for the test; they're giving their students better resources to process the world around them.

2. Do you aim for resolution instead of increasing wonder?

   Our instinct is almost always to seek resolution and move on, but that is not the only path toward learning. Remember in the book of Job when Job asked God why so many good people suffer so much evil? God's response wasn't to give Job simple answers to his questions. It was to increase Job's sense of wonder, reminding him of God's vastness and power and humanity's limited understanding. We need to be able to sit in uncertainty and wonder with an open mind and no preconceived notions. In this way, we can create a sense of mystery that will keep people coming back for more.

3. Do you define boundaries instead of imagining what's beyond them?

There is a difference between teaching the truth and just defining boundaries. The truth sets us free. Teaching people the truth sparks creativity and imagination. But boundaries act as barriers to creativity and imagination. We must break free from these barriers and try to think beyond the realm of only what is established and well known. By doing so, we can push the envelope and ultimately foster a culture of imagination and innovation that speaks to the heart of the curious.

It's not just our preaching and teaching that gets impacted by our predilection toward certainty. Consider the artwork that adorns many of our churches. Most of it is simple, straightforward, and concrete; it is obvious what is being depicted.

But have you ever seen Barnett Newman's *Stations of the Cross*? I had the opportunity to see it when it was on display at the National Gallery of Art in Washington, DC. After spending several hours viewing the exhibit, I returned to DC for another visit just to view it again.

Newman's abstract interpretation of the stations of the cross comprises fourteen huge canvases, each of them painted a single color fringed by narrow bands, what Newman called "zips," of another color. The series does not follow a linear narrative. Instead, Newman approaches each station as a separate entity, addressing various aspects of Christ's passion. To experience the stations, one needs to stand in front of each painting in a sequence to understand the series' impact as a whole. The colors are limited and create an arresting presence. Despite the lack of figurative representation, Newman's interpretation seeks to capture the essence of each station's emotional and spiritual moment. The size of the paintings also offers a visual experience that requires the viewer to contemplate elements beyond the figurative representation of the stations of the cross. Viewing them was a powerful experience.

Or think of our music. Obviously, Christian music has a rich history, and even today, many Christian musicians are creating great songs. However, many of us seem to prefer songs with straightforward music that rarely push us to imagine beyond things we already know.

On his 1999 album *Mule Variations*, Tom Waits has a song called "Georgia Lee." It's about the unsolved murder of twelve-year-old Georgia Leah Moses. "Why wasn't God watching? Why wasn't God listening?" sings Waits on the haunting chorus. Instead of seeking to resolve these questions with any simplistic truisms, Waits sits in the tragedy and the mystery, and he invites us to sit with him. Is it uncomfortable? Very. Is it sad? Without question. But it's also a deeply human experience.

Why isn't art like this more prominent in churches today?

I would suggest that perhaps we have created a "cognitive culture" that favors those with a higher need for closure. By "cognitive culture," I mean a shared set of values, practices, rhythms, and objectives that help us resolve the tension that exists in an increasingly complex world. If our cognitive culture values certainty and closure rather than curiosity and openness, then the very environment and experience we produce will likely appeal less to those who have different preferences than we have. Obviously, there is nothing wrong with appealing to people with a higher need for closure. I am only arguing that we are doing so a little too well—often to the detriment of people with a lower need for closure and a higher proclivity for curiosity.

But appealing to the Spiritually Curious isn't the only reason to think beyond this cognitive culture. My hope as we dive deeper into what it means to be spiritually curious is that we might not only learn how to better lead others to a saving relationship with Christ but that we too might discover something more that we have been missing in our own spiritual experiences.

What about Christians with a lower need for closure? Yes, there are Christians with a low need for closure too. You might recognize them as troublemakers in your church, always trying to rattle the status quo. They're asking uncomfortable questions. They might come across as too critical or too skeptical. But often these people aren't trying to rock the boat or be a pesky thorn in the side of the leadership. Maybe they're using words like "deconstruct" to describe their faith journey. If you've been paying attention, you may now understand them (or yourself, if I'm talking about you!) a little better. These Christians aren't necessarily trying to cause problems; they may just be bored or trying to make room for expressions that are more authentic for them.

Ambiguity, risk, and uncertainty are stimulants that give life to people with a low need for closure. The Christians some might view as troublemakers may actually be trying to scratch a fundamental itch in their personality. Since these Christians are a statistical minority in their churches, they may often feel alone or self-conscious about this impulse. Maybe they squash it, burying their true nature so they don't cause any problems. In some cases, they may decide they just don't belong in church. When we stigmatize spiritual curiosity, we miss opportunities for spiritual connection with a huge and vital portion of our local communities.

5

A Curious Posture

In the last few years, many churches have not seen a return to pre-pandemic attendance. Where are all of those who attended, and what are they doing with their time? My guess is that there are different reasons people aren't coming back, and our "cognitive culture" could be part of it.

Whenever new territories open up or new ideas emerge on society's frontier, people adapt to process the change. I'd say that the Spiritually Curious and Curious Skeptic are two mindsets that have increased dramatically as a result of digital Babylon's impact on society. We see the spread of these mentalities outside the church; obviously, people in our pews are also reacting to this tectonic shift. By examining the data on Practicing Christians, we can identify two frames of mind that Christians adopt to navigate digital Babylon and the ambiguity of spiritual openness. They are the Pioneer and the Settler archetypes.

Practicing Christians as Pioneers or Settlers: How They View Uncertainty

Read each of the following statements and decide how much you agree with each according to your beliefs and experiences.
% strongly agree

● Pioneer   ● Settler

Statement	Pioneer	Settler
I feel irritated when one person disagrees with what everyone else in a group believes	2%	24%
I dislike questions that could be answered in many different ways	2%	30%
I feel uncomfortable when I don't understand the reason why an event occured in my life	4%	35%
I dislike unpredictable situations	4%	40%
I would quickly become impatient and irritated if I would not find a solution to a problem immediately	5%	20%
I do not usually consult many different opinions before forming my own view	5%	22%
I dislike it when a person's statement could mean many different things	5%	30%
I don't like to be with people who are capable of unexpected actions	7%	41%
I don't like situations that are uncertain	9%	40%
I don't like to go into a situation without knowing what I can expect from it	10%	49%
When I am confronted with a problem, I'm anxious to reach a solution very quickly	11%	32%
I find that a well-ordered life with regular hours suits my temperament	16%	41%
I find that establishing a consistent routine enables me to enjoy life more	20%	46%
When I have made a decision, I feel relieved	30%	50%
I enjoy having a clear and structured mode of life	32%	53%

n=287 U.S. Practicing Christian adults, February 19–23, 2023. Source: Barna Group

The Pioneer embraces the changes and challenges brought on by digital Babylon, seeing it as a wild and untamed frontier to be explored. On the other hand, the Settler chooses to establish a "homestead," staking out a plot to call their own where they can feel safe and secure.

It's important to remember that these are just two different mindsets, and neither is better or worse than the other. Each archetype has certain strengths and weaknesses and can be used for either good or bad. However, if a church aims to connect with the curious, it must be mindful of any limitations its dominant culture might impose on outreach efforts. Take a look at the preceding chart, which represents Practicing Christians divided by their openness to uncertainty. The Settlers are the light blue bars. The Pioneers are the dark blue ones.

My contention is that the Settler mindset is the dominant culture of our churches. If we want to grow as a body of believers, we need to find a way to expand our reach and make room for the Pioneers—those who are more comfortable with questions, ambiguity, and tension. People with a Pioneer mindset have much to offer to our churches, and when we learn how to accept them, there is just no telling how far we will all go together.

Curiosity That Is Open

There are two types of curiosity: curiosity seeking closure and curiosity that is open.

Early theories of curiosity focused on the discomfort we experience when we don't have a piece of information. Missing information was the motivating force that produced a curious activity. People were curious because there was something they didn't know. Once they knew it, they stopped being curious. This is curiosity seeking closure.

But later researchers explored curiosity as proactive, positive, experience-seeking, even thrill-seeking. Many people's curiosity isn't a wrinkle that needs to be smoothed. It's an experience they enjoy for its own sake. They simply enjoy living in a state of curiosity. This is curiosity that is open.

If finding new or missing information is a main catalyst for curiosity, then the same can be true for the motivation for certainty. We're driven to find information that will reduce ambiguity.

The research seems to indicate that our quest for certainty is also a quest for closure, and while therapists tell us that there isn't anything wrong with wanting this, it can lead to some negative outcomes. I'm concerned that as we experience digital Babylon, the practice of Christianity (and other religions) could be seen, by curious people, as too simplistic a solution and one that is only sought after by those trying to alleviate the discomfort of changing times.

A significant theme in this book is that the church struggles to engage those who are curious. Yet many could say it was their curiosity that originally led them to Christianity and church. We must make a distinction between curiosity that is seeking closure and curiosity that is open. A curiosity that seeks closure is a quest for certainty. While there is nothing wrong with seeking certainty (of this, I'm certain!), we must be careful to not allow the desire for certainty to resolve itself too quickly.

Dr. Todd Kashdan, who we were introduced to in chapter 2 as a leading researcher in the field of curiosity, explains it like this: "In the absence of curiosity and openness to experiences, people show an intolerance of uncertainty and a strong need for closure in their lives. While these characteristics might aid in protecting a person from anxiety and stress, their destructive influences on social relationships are far-ranging. Less curious people rely on stereotypes to describe others and find new information inconsistent with these beliefs to be threatening."[1]

In churches dominated by people with a high need for closure and a high prioritization of certainty, this can be a disaster. If someone shares our views, we praise them. If someone questions or challenges our views, we criticize, attack, and discount them. The Spiritually Curious, indulging their natural impulse to ask questions and explore possibilities, suddenly find themselves on the defensive. They are characterized as a threat, a person stirring up the pot.

Lack of curiosity is a breeding ground for

- stereotyping and discrimination that in the extreme leads to hatred and even violence,
- inflated confidence and ignorance that leads to poor decisions, and
- dogmatism and rigid thinking, which is the opposite of psychological flexibility.

In some ways, the last decade has seen an increase of incidents of Christian leadership doubling down on certainty. It's happened politically, theologically, and ecumenically. Many churches have tightened their ranks, growing more wary of uncertainty instead of more open to curiosity.

Kashdan warns, "We need to be wary of the need for certainty. Seeking certitude can cause our beliefs and decision making to crystallize prematurely, and the resulting reluctance to consider new information can hurt us in the long run. From the research on this topic, we know the sad irony that the greater a person's need for certainty, the more confident they are that their ideas are 'right.'"[2]

While Kashdan's remarks are not at all aimed at the church or Christianity, it isn't hard to see how they relate. In our search for truth, the Christian faith can bring satisfaction to the unknowns of life. But a premature closure to our understanding—an internal notion that we've pretty much figured it out—has the potential to lead us into a lesser experience of the Trinity in our daily lives. It could lead us to judge and belittle our fellow humans rather than to engage in the deep expressions of love Christ commanded toward even our enemies. We see people with a lower need for closure as a threat to our own faith instead of someone who simply has a different way of exploring faith than we do.

Deconstruction Junction, What's Your Function?

When a Christian becomes curious in a culture of certainty, they can find they have no safe place to explore their questions. The people they have come to consider family, in a culture that values closure, often don't know how to respond to them. This can lead to doubts and then a need to restructure the foundation of their understanding of Christianity. This is a maturing process for most Christians, but some communities of faith can't handle the doubts and questions of their brothers and sisters, leaving individuals feeling alone, rejected, disoriented, and disillusioned. This phenomenon has been called "deconstructing" by some.

Christians do not need to be skeptical or judgmental of those who say they are "deconstructing" their faith. Instead, we can recognize that they are going through an important process of exploring their assumptions and following their natural inclination to better understand what they believe and why. And we can come alongside them, in grace and humility, to help them in their journey and make space in our communities for their exploration.

Let's imagine a young woman named Carrie. Carrie was raised in a conservative Christian home, gave her life to Jesus at a young age, and spent her middle school and high school years as a dedicated student leader in the youth group, frequenting Wednesday night Bible studies and summer mission trips. As Carrie came of age, she started paying attention to the world around her. Like many people her age, Carrie grew concerned by frequent stories of unchecked police brutality, particularly against Black people. She also grew uncomfortable with certain political figures who claimed Christian faith on the one hand but whose behavior and policies seemed to be at odds with biblical teaching.

These things along with several related factors sent Carrie on a spiritual journey of reevaluating the Christian beliefs she grew up with. Note that Carrie isn't questioning her belief in God or her faith in Jesus. These foundational elements of her faith remain secure. However, she is growing more curious about some of the biblical interpretations she's been raised to believe, along with the social implications of those beliefs.

This is that process some have come to call *deconstruction*. This broad term can encompass a wide range of spiritual journeys. Some may be considerably more dramatic than Carrie's, with lifelong Christians questioning their belief in Jesus or abandoning Christianity altogether. Others may be more nuanced, with Christians rethinking smaller details of the faith. Whatever this process looks like, it can be very frightening and lonely for Christians who practice their faith in high-certainty environments.

Let's return to Carrie. Let's say she takes some of her questions to trusted older Christians in her church. Let's say she expresses outrage about stories she's seen of police shooting unarmed Black people. Let's say she expresses her disappointment when respected Christian leaders support politicians who behave in un-Christian ways.

This is a crucial point in Carrie's deconstruction process. If the trusted Christian leaders react to her with judgment, defensiveness, or outrage, the lesson Carrie will most likely learn is that the church is not a place for people like her. It will be her understanding that no questions are allowed in Christianity, and the cherished community she's grown up with has accepted her only on the condition that she unquestioningly swallow every last spoonful she is fed.

It should go without saying that this is not fertile soil in which a strong, robust faith can flourish. If Carrie does stay in the church, her beliefs will be rooted in fear. She will suppress asking questions about things that are important to her. Her faith will be like a house of cards—outwardly intricate but easily knocked over. It will not take much to bring Carrie's faith crashing down.

It's very likely that Carrie will not remain in the church, sensing that she and her questions are unwelcome. Perhaps she'll decide that the Christians she's always assumed had a robust faith have no deep roots at all and fear any questions or doubt. At this point, her limited deconstruction process may go into turbo drive. After all, if the people who taught her to believe in Jesus can't handle a few questions, why should they be trusted with the big questions of life and meaning? Why should anyone be surprised if Carrie takes her questions elsewhere, to people outside the Christian faith who show an interest in hearing her out?

Indeed, this may explain the exodus we've seen from the church among young people, who went looking for ways to explore their faith and found themselves cut off at every question. The Christians who refused to entertain the curiosity of people like Carrie may have thought they were doing them a favor, herding them away from a "slippery slope." But in reality they were pushing them down a different slope that also led them astray.

What if, instead, Carrie's questions were not met with alarm, judgment, or defensiveness but with mutual curiosity? What if the older Christians she turned to asked her questions in response, seeking to understand more about Carrie's beliefs and feelings instead of just assuming they already understood all there was to know about her curiosity? What if they helped her connect her questions to God's heart for all people in a way that invited Carrie deeper into fellowship with the church instead of pushing her away?

When this happens, deconstruction just becomes the first step in a process of "reconstruction"—rebuilding a young, flimsy faith into something sturdy and resilient, able to withstand the storms of life. Carrie now knows that she can bring her natural curiosity to her faith community and that the journey she's on isn't something she has to do alone. She has trusted guides who can listen to her questions, connect her to resources, and walk with her down the road ahead. They can even learn from her, understanding that God is speaking to all of us, and some of the things he has been teaching her may very well be things the rest of the church needs to hear. Fostering curiosity is not only good for the Spiritually Curious, it benefits the entire church.

Strictly speaking, Carrie is hypothetical. But the reality is that men and women just like Carrie are in your church. They are filled with questions, but they are afraid to speak up. They intuitively understand that they are in a high-closure culture, and they are protecting themselves by playing along. But if we work to make our churches safe places for spiritually curious Christians to open up about their questions, we will be astonished at how many take us up on the offer—and see their faith deepen as a result.

The Case for More Mystery

We must be honest with ourselves about our need for closure if we want to have a resilient faith. Premature certitude does not build a strong foundation but rather a fragile one. If something is not fully formed, it takes very little to knock it down.

One very easy place to observe all this is the ongoing "debate" between what the Bible says and what scientific inquiry teaches. Because of the tension between Scripture and science, I have seen many young people stray from faith to disbelief, when nothing of the sort needed to happen. It is entirely possible to have full confidence in the Scriptures without dismissing modern science out of hand. The Bible itself gives us tools for this attitude.

One of the unique qualities of Hebrew wisdom is the limits it places on human knowledge and understanding, which are primarily explored in Ecclesiastes and, once again, the book of Job. Job's friends, and even Job himself, assume that living a virtuous life leads to happiness and prosperity. Yet this is clearly not the case. Job's friends assume he has done something wrong. Why else would he be facing so much misfortune? But Job knows he has not sinned against God. It is only when Job is in debate with God that God reveals not everything can be understood by the human mind. Despite all that has been revealed in nature, and subsequently in Scripture, we still see through a glass dimly.

For Christians, God's admonition to Job is a good reminder to maintain intellectual humility and avoid the hubris that pushes people away from the faith. Sometimes the answer to our biggest questions is not more certainty but more mystery.

So we have two information-seeking trajectories: one that is motivated by closure and the other that is open. Given this, you can see why we might misinterpret what kind of quest the curious person is on and what they're really looking for. Our misunderstanding leads to errors like those that follow.

We Mistake the Search of the Curious to Be Finite

Those who are curious but aren't motivated by closure are typically curious about many things. They're like butterflies that land on a topic for a moment and then are off to another subject. On the other hand, if closure is the objective, it becomes the sole mission of an individual to bring their exploration to a definitive end. They're more like badgers who won't stop burrowing until they find what they're looking for.

Anika, the spiritually curious individual introduced at the beginning of this book, was deeply engrossed in our discussion until her attention shifted elsewhere. Something new captivated her interest, and it did not bother her that the previous conversation hadn't reached any real conclusion. For her, that particular moment held enough fulfillment.

Later, I extended an invitation to continue our spiritual exploration conversation. She never pursued it. It wasn't because she resented me or didn't enjoy our previous conversation—she had simply moved on to explore other topics. Thankfully, our paths crossed once more. At our next encounter, I made a conscious choice to nurture curiosity in other aspects of her life, which led to deeper engagement.

If you aren't genuinely interested in pursuing life with a spiritually curious person, it won't work; you have to care about more than just the spiritual part of their journey.

We Mistake the Search of the Curious to Be about Finding an Expert or Authority Who Has Solved the Problem

If you're a person looking for closure, finding an authority or expert—a person with credentials—is a top priority. Sometimes, getting an expert opinion can be enough to complete the discovery process. But curious people aren't likely to find the authority of Scripture to be enough, in and of itself, for them to accept it. Will they be interested to hear from someone with expertise on a topic? Yes, very much so.

But they tend to be more interested in self-validation. So, an actual experience with the Bible will likely go much further than simple proof texting. I've often found that providing counterevidence from other authorities against my position is helpful. Offering curious individuals the option to explore alternative perspectives engages their interest in looking at all sides of an issue. They enjoy hearing different opinions. By appealing to their innate curiosity, we open doors for deeper engagement and potentially transformative experiences.

We Mistakenly Think We Need to Close the Deal

When I get to heaven, I will be curious to find out what ended up happening to the rich young ruler in the Gospels. Did he ever come around to placing his trust in Jesus? In all my fifty-some years of going to church, almost every sermon I've heard on the ruler strongly implied that he probably walked away from Jesus for good and went to hell when he died.

And maybe that's what we're supposed to assume. But let me offer another possibility. Maybe Jesus was demonstrating the importance of being cognizant of the journey of discovery a person is on. We know Jesus loved this rich young ruler. We also know he didn't run after this ruler and beg him to stick around. Maybe Jesus just understood that trust takes time to firmly develop. The young man walked away, but maybe not forever. Jesus had shifted this man's paradigm and challenged his assumptions. Jesus wasn't interested in cheap, easy beliefism, and he was willing to give this young man space to process this new information. He left the door open for further spiritual conversation. If we trust Jesus, we should be okay doing the same.

We Make It Too Difficult to Trust in Jesus

There are many cautions about being careful not to lead others astray or cause them to stumble. These passages are severe, like Jesus's words in Matthew: "If anyone causes one of these little ones—those who believe in me—to stumble, it would be better for them to have a large millstone hung around their neck and to be drowned in the depths of the sea" (18:6).

Sometimes we become so concerned about doing Christian life the right way that we make it intimidating for novices to even try. We're like figure skaters who expect others to land a triple axel the first time they lace up a pair of skates. Even though we don't consciously believe they have to change their behaviors or believe specific theological concepts to be a true Christian, we sure behave that way, even unintentionally. We put a high burden on people to mimic our own beliefs and behaviors to a T rather than allow their simple, childlike trust to mature over time.

In Mark 10:14–15, Jesus also said of children, in a rebuke to his disciples, "Let the little children come to me, and do not hinder them, for the kingdom of God belongs to such as these. Truly I tell you, anyone who will not receive the kingdom of God like a little child will never enter it."

Who is more curious than a child? But older, more mature adults might argue that children are asking too many questions, don't yet have all their intellectual faculties, and need more foundation so that they'll stop pestering the grownups. And some more mature, certainty-oriented believers say the same of the Spiritually Curious. In Acts, as gentiles are coming to faith and being filled with the Spirit, a controversy breaks out. What do the gentiles have to do now that they are

Christians? Up to that point, the early church had been made up almost entirely of Jewish believers. Should the new gentile believers adopt Jewish practices? James's reply is clear: "It is my judgment, therefore, that we should not make it difficult for the Gentiles who are turning to God" (15:19).

He advises them of a few cultural practices that would be good for them to observe for their own benefit and to keep the peace in the community. But these practices aren't challenging, nor are they barriers to becoming part of the faith. We too should not make it unnecessarily difficult for the Spiritually Curious to access Jesus.

What Curiosity Requires

I hope you are seeing that part of reaching the curious is becoming more curious ourselves. Having a curiosity about the lives and spiritual pilgrimages of others helps us to better and more honestly engage with them. Having a deep curiosity about God will lead us to spend increased time with him, leading to greater intimacy in our relationship with him. Having general curiosity about the world shows humility and an acknowledgment that there will always be more to learn. Curiosity requires . . .

Awareness of Assumptions, Boundaries, and Limitations

Sometimes we don't know what else is out there until we approach the fence. The more we are conscious of our assumptions, the more we can find space for curiosity. Some of the Pharisees Jesus interacted with clearly lacked curiosity. While some, like Nicodemus, were quite curious, other Pharisees had made many assumptions, set many boundaries, and created limitations that actually hindered their quest for holiness instead of helping it. They had so many rules about how to find the Messiah that they missed him entirely when they had their chance.

I grew up in a rural city in Southern California. We didn't live far from Los Angeles, but that city—with its cosmopolitan influence and hotbed of culture—might as well have been another planet. My parents didn't listen to the radio, and television was fairly limited. Our lives were filled with activities and relationships related to church. Even though my parents never spoke much of these things, I was very uncomfortable around alcohol and rock music when I was in elementary school. I remember walking into a teachers lounge once and saw most of the teachers smoking like chimneys. I lost respect for most of them immediately. The same was true for adults who drank alcohol, something I rarely witnessed until I became close friends with a family down the street.

This family didn't pray before meals, drank wine, and listened to rock. They also went to movies much more frequently than we did. While my parents had a significant influence on me, so did this family. I learned about culture, the arts, and entertainment from them. Once, when I was in elementary school, I remember questioning the evil of alcohol in their home and they just laughed at me. (I'm lucky they didn't kick me out; I was one judgmental little kid!)

I learned through my teenage years that I had certain assumptions about life that had limited my understanding of God, myself, and others. I also had boundaries I'd put in place that limited my experiences and comfort zones. Sometimes my lack of curiosity didn't come from real conviction.

It came from fear of what I might discover if I started to explore.

Approaching the Known and Unknown with Courage and Humility

If God is on our side, who can be against us? When Jesus invited the disciples to "come, follow me, . . . and I will send you out to fish for people" (Matt. 4:19), I'm fairly certain they had no idea what he was talking about.

Their sense of curiosity led them to drop their nets and follow him. He took them to different towns, to "the other side." He led them to break the Sabbath and associate with outcasts. And had they not, Peter might never have declared that Jesus was the Christ. They would never have seen miracles performed.

The disciples' decision took courage, but that courage also required a certain humility. That same balance of courage and humility is required from us. To become truly wise, we need to understand the limits of our knowledge. We need to trust (and be okay with) God as the only one who is in control.

An Appeal to Wonder

When something disrupts you or confuses you, how are you most likely to respond? Many of us rush to resolution—glancing over any complexities along the way—but does that actually aid our growth?

In our divided world, we often draw easy, one-dimensional conclusions about people who think differently than us rather than ask, "I wonder why they believe that? I wonder what makes them take that position?" We fail to assume that their reasons for believing what they do are probably just as nuanced and complicated as our own.

This approach isn't about compromising our beliefs. It is about trying to look deeper into another person's life and experiences to get to know them and the reasons they may think certain ways about certain things.

Realizing That While Truth May Be the Desired Goal, the Journey—Not the Destination—Is Formational

In some ways, Christians are almost hardwired to jump to certainty over curiosity. As we'll discuss further in chapter 7 (see the chart on p. 159), Christians, especially Practicing Christians, are significantly more likely to say they are "comfortable and certain about their beliefs" than that they are "compelled to dig deeper to learn more about what [they] believe" or "content that [they] don't have all the answers." And the gap between their certainty and a compulsion to dig deep or contentment with not having all the answers is significantly wider than it is among Curious Skeptics or the Spiritually Curious. I believe this is because we hold "truth" to be central to our faith.

Yet for truth to change us, we must do more than just mentally assent to it. It is the journey of the curious that leads to true transformation, and that may take some time. Sometimes, the struggle to understand truth is the process that actually changes us. Biblical wisdom makes it clear that there are limits to humanity's understanding of truth. While truth can set us free (John 8:32), Job reminds us that God has not made all truth known, nor is it our right to access it. This doesn't mean that truth doesn't exist nor that we shouldn't strive to know the truth, only that we should have the humility to remember we will never grasp all of it on this side of eternity.

In fact, the Bible teaches that God enjoys crafting mysteries so that we can enjoy the process of exploring them. Proverbs 25:2 says, "It is the glory of God to conceal a matter; to search out a matter is the glory of kings." When we "search out a matter," we are participating in the glory of God in a profound way. And while our quest for truth may reveal many answers about our Creator, we should always remember that we will never know everything on this side of eternity. As 1 Corinthians 13:12 says, "For now we see only a reflection as in a mirror; then we shall see face to face. Now I know in part; then I shall know fully, even as I am fully known."

Recognizing That Curiosity Doesn't Compromise Convictions

"Curiosity killed the cat." The implication, of course, is that curiosity is a dangerous personality flaw. This familiar bit of conventional wisdom has prevented generations from ever exploring the majesty and breadth of God's creation and the wonder of who we are made to be in his image.

If everything that is true belongs to God, then we don't need to fear curiosity. Curiosity only seeks out what is true, so we can trust that any serious quest will never stray far from the Author of all truth. I was often told there were certain places and experiences that I should avoid for fear that my convictions would fail. "Don't get too close to the fire or else you'll get burned," says the common adage.

Certainly there is wisdom in being thoughtful about what environments we choose to be in. But sadly, we have been so afraid of "getting burned" that we avoid places that spiritually curious people might frequent. We are so afraid of even the appearance of evil that we won't fraternize with those searching for what we claim to have already found.

Remember Jesus . . .

Matthew tells us, "The Son of Man came eating and drinking, and they say, 'Here is a glutton and a drunkard, a friend of tax collectors and sinners.' But wisdom is proved right by her deeds" (11:19). Jesus did not let a fear of being associated with rowdy behavior keep him from connecting with the Spiritually Curious. Being open to curiosity will challenge your assumptions, boundaries, and limitations. It might be uncomfortable. It will certainly make others uncomfortable. But it will also take you into a deeper encounter with Jesus, the people he died to save, and his mission.

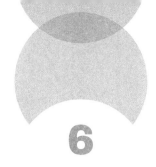

6

Engaging the Spiritually Curious

As Christians, we have the opportunity to engage the Spiritually Curious in meaningful conversations about faith. One of the best ways to do this is by learning how to ask what I call *spiritual discovery questions*. These questions help us behave in a curious way toward other people, allowing them to lead their own journey. It also is an opportunity to break some of our conditioned thinking about non-Christians and their assumptions about us as Christians.

May I Pray for You?

In my early twenties, Phil Newberry, a friend and youth pastor at Bellevue Baptist in Memphis, Tennessee, first modeled for me what a good spiritual discovery question looks like. We had met up for lunch, and after placing our order and having some friendly banter with our waitress, Crystal, Phil boldly said to her, "Crystal, Mark and I are going to pray for our food when it comes. Is there anything you might like us to pray about for you?"

I just about fell out of my chair at his boldness. But then what really floored me was seeing Crystal tear up. She went on to tell us that she knew she needed to end things with her boyfriend but was struggling with how to break the relationship off. One simple question gave us a window into her deepest point of pain and offered her a moment of genuine care from two strangers.

I experienced this same phenomenon with Phil many times. Sometimes people opened up about deep pains and struggles. Sometimes they would request little more than prayer for a loved one who was sick. But I never saw anyone refuse prayer.

Once, when I asked a waiter this question on my own, without Phil, he told me he couldn't think of anything to pray for. However, when he later returned with the check, he said, "I couldn't think of anything when you asked me. I've never had anyone ask to pray for me. I saw that you already did but, if you pray again, would you pray for an exam I have coming up on Friday?" My offers to pray have never failed to get a welcome response.

Now, I don't offer to pray as often as Phil did (maybe I should!), but what I learned from him was that most people are not hostile to spiritual engagement. In fact, just the opposite. They often open up.

Spiritual Engagement

I want to explore some unique frames for engaging the Spiritually Curious, but the first consideration is addressing the source of their curiosity.

Remember my conversation with Anika in chapter 1? Did you notice that when I shared the gospel, I used an image of a broken mirror to communicate how sin destroyed our relationship with God and our ability to reflect him, to make his character known?

We believe that all people are made in the image of God, but sin has disrupted the ability to be an image bearer. God's image in us is like a shattered mirror, but there are "shards" that reflect God's character, even if imperfectly. When a spiritually curious person connects with these shards, they feel the sensation of doing what they were made for, and that can make some want to experience more. We see examples of this everywhere we look.

They feel God's compassion and want to care for those who are hurting.

They feel God's righteousness and want to stand against injustice, righting wrongs.

They feel God's peace and want to reconcile people who are fighting against one another.

We might call this an expression of "redemptive curiosity"—people exercising God's character by connecting with the fragments of his image in them, possibly without even realizing it. They may be aware that the few shards they've collected aren't enough—that there must be a way to piece these shards back together into a complete mirror—but the condition of sin has destroyed their capacity to fully do this.

And so we see the world attempt to do good apart from God, which inevitably falls short.

Defining Sin

It's really difficult to talk about Christianity without talking about sin, and I find many Christians struggle with defining sin. Maybe this is because we're working with several different definitions of the word. Given America's Christian heritage, many people have wildly different understandings about what sin even is. It creates a lot of confusion.

When most think of sin, they think of certain taboo behaviors that are considered by God—or a group of people—to be out of bounds. The list of sins is numerous, and there's no definitive, exhaustive list of every single thought and behavior we need to avoid. And there is no question that our human selves place different weight on different sins as well. There are "big" sins like murder and stealing, of course. But there are also "smaller" sins, like lying, lust, and gossip. What about exceptions, like killing in self-defense or lying to protect someone, which many brave Germans who hid Jewish families from the Nazis in Germany did during World War II? And that's even before we get into issues about whether an act is old covenant or new covenant. And what about behaviors that exist today that aren't even mentioned in the Scriptures?

We know that some Pharisees—in their pursuit of holiness—wrestled with these things too, defining many purity laws to help the pious live the best they could. But that all fell apart, didn't it? These Pharisees misunderstood sin, grace, and Jesus himself even when he was right there next to them.

For all these reasons, we need to move beyond thinking of sin as a simple list of dos and don'ts. We have to consider what we think about sin as we craft our message to the Spiritually Curious. Because they have ideas about it too.

Here is an approach to framing sin that I've found helpful in engaging the Spiritually Curious on this topic:

Move from Portraying Sin as a "List of Behaviors" to Describing It as a Condition

When introducing Christ to the spiritually neutral, the condition of sin is the most important discussion. Many spiritually curious people think of morality as a giant set of scales in the sky, where good and bad deeds will one day be weighed and each person will be judged accordingly. Based on the perspective the individual holds on life after death, their next thoughts may vary as to how this judgment will impact their reincarnation, stance in the afterlife, or other future state. This idea is unhelpful though, and it's not how the Bible talks about sin. I want them to see sin as a condition, not a scenario leading to a ratio of good to bad works.

Affirm Positive Connections with the Spiritually Curious's Motivation toward Spirituality

It's easy to focus on the negative—how sin has separated us from God. But talking about sin as a condition also points us toward the Good News: the image of God in us all may be broken, but it is by no means lost for good. Connecting their curiosity about spirituality with the image of God in them helps the Spiritually Curious understand how they fit into the garden of Eden story and why they need Jesus. They want to be able to reflect the image of God they have seen. (Just wait until they meet him!)

Frame Sin Using Relational Theology

The fall of humanity was a destroyer of our relationships—with God, other people, creation, and our own selves. This is very clear with even a cursory understanding of the story of the fall in Genesis. That's a story I've never had anyone have a problem with. Even if they decide Jesus isn't who they trust in for hope, they see what Jesus has done through his death and resurrection in a new light. Sin then, whether a condition or a specific behavior, is the destroyer of relationships.

Remember, for younger generations, relationships are *everything*. Using relational language to explain sin and redemption is speaking to them in their first language.

Frame Redemption as the Antidote for Sin

While there is a legal element in understanding atonement, we have made the legal aspect paramount and missed the relational aspect of redemption. We've all heard preachers say, "Jesus isn't offering you a 'Get Out of Hell Free Card'; he's offering you a relationship with him." This is very true, but it raises a question: Why do we even need to clarify this? Where did our presentation of the gospel get so far off track that so many people think of Jesus as nothing more than an escape ladder from hell?

I was always told the non-Christian is looking to fill the "hole in their soul." We seem to think that all non-Christians have a certain malaise in life that Christianity can solve for them. People may have that "hole in their soul," but in my experience, very few people are actually cognizant of it. While some people—like people who struggle with addiction, for example—may be aware of something missing in their life, it's a rare person I've led to Christ who held this attitude.

Instead of asking non-Christians to confront an existential crisis that most of them aren't actually experiencing, maybe we should ask them to explore their inner desire to do good. The world is filled with people who aren't Christians who are doing good. Perhaps it's not a hole in the soul they're longing to have filled but something broken that wants to get bigger and be restored. That broken thing is the image of God that we were all made in that is now a mere shard of God's full reflection.

Now you are beginning a conversation by finding the part of them that experiences the image of God. That's a much better way to share the Good News than starting with, "We all have sinned and upset God." Even though that is true, remember that even Paul started his message on Mars Hill by commending his audience for being spiritual people, and he told them he could help them know the unknown God (Acts 17).

The Assumptions We Can Make

Going back to my interactions with waiters (and other strangers), here are some assumptions we can make from the research about someone unknown who you may approach.

They Likely Believe There Is a Supernatural World, Even If They Don't Know What They Believe about It

When asked to rate how certain they are that there is a spiritual dimension to life, 78 percent of U.S. adults are either completely certain (42 percent) or somewhat certain

(36 percent) that there is a spiritual dimension. Barna has also found that people tend to describe their spirituality as something in development or in progress, using terms like "growing" and "open."[1] Being aware of this can give you confidence that the person you are speaking with likely believes something about spirituality and is not closed off to thinking or talking about the topic. Start there.

They Have a Spiritual Journey in Their Present or Past

Remember that 64 percent of Americans identify as a Christian and 14 percent say they are of another faith, which leaves 22 percent who say they have no faith. Yet of those 22 percent who say "none," 55 percent tell us they were raised in a Christian home (see Spiritually Open survey on p. 228). In other words, there's a high likelihood that the stranger you are approaching has a past or present spiritual journey, perhaps one that meandered through the church at some point. Just because someone may not claim Christian faith now, that doesn't mean they are wholly unfamiliar with it.

In fact, their specific familiarity may have bred contempt. A key point from Barna's research is that even spiritually open non-Christians who have a Christian background often report *very* different experiences of church than their peers who have remained devout.[2] Their past journey with Christianity didn't lead to a sense of belonging. Instead, it might have lacked vitality or opportunities for them to feel like a meaningful, contributing member of a faith community. For many, it may have even become a source of anxiety.

The person you're speaking to may know more about Christianity than you expect, and that knowledge may have come with personal challenges.

They Likely Have Some Concept of What Happens after Death but Probably No Idea What Will Happen to Them Personally

You have a 50/50 shot here. When we asked people to choose from a list of options what they believe happens when a person dies, nearly half told us they believe people will face judgment before God for their decisions made on earth.

Which one of these statements best describes your own belief about what will happen to you after you die?

	All U.S. adults	Practicing Christians	Spiritually Curious	Curious Skeptics	Naturalists
When I die, I will go to heaven because I have confessed my sins and have accepted Jesus Christ as my Savior	29%	59%	29%	18%	1%
When I die, I will go to heaven because I am basically a good person	14%	11%	13%	15%	1%
When I die, I will go to heaven because God loves all people and will not let them perish	7%	6%	8%	6%	2%
When I die, I will go to heaven because I have tried to obey the Ten Commandments	5%	10%	5%	1%	–
When I die, I will not go to heaven	4%	3%	5%	2%	9%
I do not know what will happen after I die	42%	11%	38%	58%	86%

n=1,501 U.S. adults, February 19–23, 2023. Source: Barna Group

The rest hold a range of beliefs: their spirit is reincarnated (21 percent), their spirit is terminated and ceases to exist (17 percent), or something else (17 percent). You can see the results of this discussion on the chart "How Curiosity Intersects with Views of the Afterlife" (on p. 67).

But then we asked, "Which one of these statements best describes your own belief about what will happen to you after you die?" The top response? They have no idea. Forty-two percent say they do not know what will happen to them, far exceeding the percentages who believe they will go to heaven because they trust in Jesus's death on the cross (29 percent) or because they've been a good person (14 percent). Even as people form conclusions to big questions about eternity, divine judgment, or the afterlife, they struggle to place themselves or their own futures within the answers.

They Need to Know That You Care about Them and That It Is Safe to Honestly Engage with You

While I have found few people resist authentic spiritual conversations, I am very careful to maintain my posture of discovery. I don't want to just "pretend" to be curious, like a used car salesman pretending to care so that you'll be more likely to stick around for the sales pitch. Instead, I'm genuinely curious about them. It's not a trick where once they answer my question, I can tell them what I want to say. In fact, I try not to have any predetermined outcome other than a genuine hope of continued friendship.

This means I request permission before asking a sensitive question. If I see they may be uncomfortable, I apologize for probing. And I always ask if it's okay to share my perspective or story, rather than just assume they are equally curious about me.

Proverbs 27:14 says, "If anyone loudly blesses their neighbor early in the morning, it will be taken as a curse." The idea behind this biblical adage is that *how* we engage people is important. And that if we do or say something the wrong way, that can be worse than not doing or saying anything at all. Many may have been conditioned to insert themselves where they aren't welcome when it comes to evangelism and outreach. The implication is that the Good News is too important to be overly concerned about when and how we share it, so if people aren't in the mood to hear what we have to say, then, well, too bad. I try not to think about my interactions with others in that way and am intentional about not making the opportunities I have to interact with people more about me than about them. I'm curious about the spirituality of others because spiritual matters and people are significant to me, and I want to always leave people more, not less, interested in exploring Christianity and dialoguing with Christians.

They'll Likely Find It Easier to Share Personal Stories Than to Answer Questions about Their Beliefs

A good chunk of my evangelism training has focused on asking people what they believe. I find people very willing to respectfully engage in discussions about beliefs, but it is far more interesting (and meaningful) to hear their spiritual experiences and stories. Indeed, Barna has learned that when people of no faith talk to a Christian they know about spirituality, they are more likely to report having a positive experience when there is some exchange of backstories.[3]

While it is important to discuss beliefs, I try not to lead with those questions. If I do, I will usually frame it like this: "Some people believe Jesus was God's Son and rose from the dead, others believe he was just a good teacher. Have you ever thought much about it?" Or, "When my grandmother passed away, it really made me think about what happens to a person after they die. Have you thought much about it?"

Questions for Spiritual Discovery

As you'll see in the following examples, spiritual discovery prompts can cover a wide range of topics and be personalized in a number of ways. You'll probably develop your own, but these are a few that I've used with success. The hardest part is asking them in the first place, but—wow—when you do and it goes well, spiritual conversations with strangers become second nature. You're not just sharing the Good News with others. You're cultivating your own childlike curiosity, learning more about the world around you by getting to know other people and meeting them where they are. There's no hierarchy here. We enter into these conversations with humility, recognizing that we all have a lot to gain from connecting with others.

Here are some spiritual discovery prompts to consider:

"Tell me about your tattoo."

When people make a decision to get a tattoo in a visible place, it's usually done for a reason and with great intention (and if not, that's probably an even better story). A person's permanent wearable art is a visible manifestation of many of their life choices, and I've found almost everyone loves to share their stories and showcase their tats. Often they are dripping with meaning and have deeply spiritual significance. People mark their bodies to recognize friendship, remember personal milestones, memorialize loss (*memento mori*), celebrate births, and commemorate romantic unions. When you ask a person to share about their tattoos, and they do, they are inviting you into a sacred part of their lives.

"Have you ever felt that God was pursuing you?"

My friend Eric Swanson is the master of spiritual discovery questions. One evening after meeting our waiter, Ruslan, and hearing about his ink (one of which was a Buddhist symbol that represented his spiritual journey), Eric led into a discovery question with this: "There's this story about a shepherd who is tending his sheep and one of them wanders off and gets lost. So the shepherd leaves the other sheep and goes out looking for the lost one until he finds him. It's a story in the Bible, and the Shepherd is supposed to be Jesus. Have you ever felt like that sheep? Like someone was pursuing you, trying to find you?"

Ruslan said, "Yeah. I've been feeling that way." Then he asked his shift manager if he could take a break to chat with us a little longer.

I've found that many spiritually curious people do feel haunted in a way they cannot explain. The reason they feel this way is, of course, because it's true. You may be the one to help them meet the Good Shepherd who is looking for them.

"Tell me about a person whose spiritual life you really admired."

Most people have an answer to this question. It's almost always a grandparent, and it's almost always a Christian.

Regardless, this question often leads to good conversation. And, what you learn about another person through this answer is remarkable. It reveals what they admire in others. The discussion leads to many unexpected places. What I find most notable, though, is the countenance of the person as they share about the person they admire. We soften when we talk about people we care about.

In a world where Christians are often featured in a negative way, this conversation can be a reminder that there are devoted Christians who are good. And when people are reminded of that, they might be more open to the idea that it's worth giving Jesus deeper consideration.

"You MUST be a Christian!"

That is, connect their work to Christian ideals. "You must be a Christian!"

In *Faith for Exiles*, David Kinnaman and I introduced the idea of vocational discipleship as one of five ways a new generation is following Jesus in digital Babylon.

As work in the U.S. has moved away from labor-focused work to talent-focused work, the search for finding meaning in work has become front of mind for many. The recent COVID pandemic not only brought work to our homes but gave us a chance to examine what matters most.

It's not that I think virtual work is better or that I don't want to go back to the office. It's that I'd rather be present at home instead of being present at work. If I'm going to deprive anyone with my lack of presence, I'd rather cheat my boss and coworkers than my family. Not commuting to work for an hour or more each day means more time with those I care about most.

The value of work has quickly shifted.

Of the five practices we unpacked in our research for *Faith for Exiles*, vocational discipleship was certainly one of the most "under experienced" practices in our churches today and yet was a defining characteristic of resilient discipleship. It was amazing to discover that following Jesus transformed the way people viewed the work they did.[4]

During the development of that project, I created a little game I used while traveling. If a person sitting next to me shared their vocation, my response was simply to say, "Oh, you must be a Christian!" As if their choice of work alone was a giveaway.

The responses that people had ranged from disorientation to anger. Most people were just dumbfounded and while laughing would ask me why I'd ever draw that conclusion. Then it became my job to describe why their career was linked to Christian virtues.

Here's a short list of some of the people I engaged. How would you link these occupations to Christianity?

- doctor (easy)
- cybersecurity expert
- asphalt manufacturer
- corrugated engineer (he designs cardboard boxes!)
- urban developer
- pharmaceutical representative with a PhD in gender studies

I'll give you a little spoiler on that last one. The pharmaceutical representative ended up being one of my most fascinating—and rewarding—experiences with a spiritual discovery prompt.

Putting a Prompt into Action

The day I found myself sitting next to the pharmaceutical representative was a long one. I arrived at Reagan National Airport at 5:00 a.m. for a 6:30 a.m. flight only to learn that flight had been canceled. It also happened to be the first day of many spring breaks, so the next available flight was at 6:00 p.m. from Dulles International Airport (nearly forty-five minutes away). I was tired and I just wanted to get home, but while waiting in line to get rebooked, I said to myself, *Lord, I'm going to explore this city looking for a reason why I'm delayed.*

I started by being intentionally kind to the counter agent. After all, she was also having a tough start to her day, having to deal with angry passengers. And then I went on to have a great Sunday in DC, walking the Mall and exploring the monuments.

All day, I looked and looked for a reason for my delay, starting conversations with strangers and hoping they might give me a clue. Nothing.

That night when I boarded the plane at Dulles, I found out that I'd been upgraded (something nice that the counter agent must have done because I had been kind to her). I plopped down in my comfy seat and met the man sitting next to me. I was really tired after walking the Mall, but when he told me he had a PhD in gender studies and worked for a pharmaceutical company, I had to play the game. "You must be a Christian!" I said.

"Why in hell would you say that!?" he blurted.

Let me tell you more about his job. He worked in a non-profit arm of the company providing a vaccine for a sexually transmitted disease in developing countries. The country he was returning from had an AIDS epidemic, and many men believed they could rid themselves of AIDS by having sex with a virgin. Horrific! In the process, not only was AIDS spreading, but so was the disease his vaccine could prevent.

"You're helping to save the lives of women that are being terrorized, minimizing the damage that is being done, and helping educate the population so these sex crimes won't continue," I said. "That seems like something only a Christian would commit his life to doing."

He disagreed. Christians in these countries had been working against him, believing that if they vaccinated these women, it would promote promiscuity. He wanted to know how I would apply the Bible to his occupation though. So, I started in Genesis and was able to explain that while it's true Christian teaching has been used as an excuse throughout history to oppress women, Jesus was radically for the empowerment and equal treatment of women. Moreover, the Bible takes sexual violence very seriously and has very strong words for anyone who would take advantage of a victim. My new friend was blown away. "My mom took me to church when I was a child, but I never heard anyone talk about the Bible like you just did."

Our conversation continued. In my mind, I was wrestling with the question, *Do I share the plan of salvation with him?* I'd said as much in unpacking Scripture, but I hadn't invited him to trust Jesus's death and resurrection for his own salvation. I had that feeling many of us get when sharing our faith. Then he said, "You know, Mark, when you told me you were a minister, I thought this flight was going to be nothing but you trying to convert me. As fascinating as this conversation has been, I'm so glad you didn't go there."

I responded, "I'm so glad you told me that, because I started my day at Reagan National at 5:00 a.m. with a coach ticket, and I asked God to show me the reason he was delaying me. And all day I wandered in search of the answer. Then I got on the plane to learn I'd been upgraded, and sat next to you, and figured this guy has to be the reason my day has been disrupted. I've been wrestling with whether or not to talk to you about your salvation, but now you've let me off the hook. I was right not to do it."

He looked at me, poured some Jack Daniel's from his tiny airline bottle into our ginger ales, and asked, "Well . . . if you were going to try and convert me . . . what would you have said?"

What Spiritually Open People Want from Spiritual Conversations

What I've shared about spiritual discovery prompts rings true with the research. People of no faith have clear ideas about the types of Christians they would be interested in learning from. First and foremost, they say they are hoping to interact with Christians who listen without judgment. They describe people who are honest about doubts, resist forced conclusions, and care about conversation partners as people.

No Judgment: The Key to Faith Conversations

Imagine a Christian you would be interested in learning from. Which of the following characteristics would you use to describe them? Select all that apply.
Base: Those of no faith

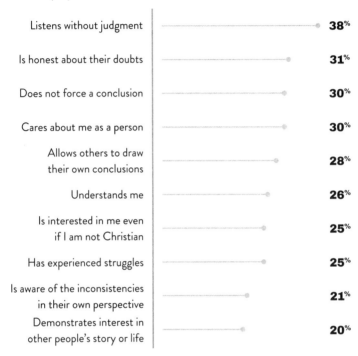

Listens without judgment	**38%**
Is honest about their doubts	**31%**
Does not force a conclusion	**30%**
Cares about me as a person	**30%**
Allows others to draw their own conclusions	**28%**
Understands me	**26%**
Is interested in me even if I am not Christian	**25%**
Has experienced struggles	**25%**
Is aware of the inconsistencies in their own perspective	**21%**
Demonstrates interest in other people's story or life	**20%**

n=412 U.S. teens and adults of no faith, December 13–22, 2022. Only the top 10 responses are shown. Source: Barna Group

Think about these qualities in light of the last story I shared:

- **Listen without judgment.**
  When my seat companion shared about his profession, I didn't make any judgments about him. Rather I admired him and made a connection to a virtue of the Christian faith. I had no need to judge him.

My goal was to introduce him to the Judge, through Jesus, who already paid the fine with his blood. I had good news to share.

- **Do not force a conclusion.**

  I was wrestling with this. How should I "land the plane," so to speak? But my objective wasn't transactional. I recognized that I was only one encounter in this man's spiritual journey, and God will be faithful to continue what he started. We, as Christians, must remember to trust the process and not behave as if everything depends on us.

- **Allow others to draw their own conclusions.**

  Ultimately, I allowed my neighbor to draw his own conclusion. He invited me to share the gospel with him. Granted, this doesn't often happen (I tell this same story frequently for a reason), but it requires having confidence in the working of the Holy Spirit and the truth of the gospel to work in due time.

These findings are also consistent with the 2019 Reviving Evangelism study that we did with Alpha.

Make It a Dialogue

The best environments for connection and learning are marked by curiosity and consideration. Barna has seen that people of no faith are more likely to have positive responses to spiritual conversations that are "exactly that: a true conversation, one where dialogue (even across differences) is embraced. In these scenarios, stories are shared, *and* questions are asked. The Christian speaks well of both their own faith community *and* the beliefs of others. There is a spirit of conversational generosity, evident in inviting the other person to participate in spiritual practices or disciplines, to talk about how they personally experience God or to help meet the needs of the other. More than anything, positive spiritual conversations are likely to be ones where Christians *listen well*."[5]

Unfortunately, Barna's research shows that few respondents describe the Christians they know or the faith discussions they have as possessing these qualities. What is more, practicing Christians themselves are hesitant to personally identify with these characteristics.[6] We have some work to do.

Yet churches can help to model and foster judgment-free spaces where honest spiritual conversations can take place. Here are some ideas for church leaders that might help you define and develop such environments for your own context:

- **Teach your congregation that Jesus was a great conversationalist.**

  During a sermon, you might highlight how Jesus listened to others and engaged them in loving, non-judgmental ways. You could also share a story from your own life of how you interacted with someone well or were heard in a way that helped you feel understood. Teachings could also address specific ways and steps to listening well. For instance, you might talk about what active listening is like and how congregants can practice these skills.

- **Encourage everyone to hold the sanctuary as a safe space.**

  It's important to understand that relational baggage, complicated cultural dynamics, and even trauma may follow people into a sanctuary, small group, or conversation. A safe space for conversation should also be a space that has grounded knowledge of mental, emotional, and relational well-being and is sensitive toward possible differences across races, ethnicities, religions, cultures, genders, and generations.

- **Develop some interesting questions.**

  Integrate good questions and icebreakers into the culture of your church. There are now many popular "conversation card games" or apps that are specifically developed to help people go deeper and build relationships. Could similarly thoughtful prompts and reflections show up (even on physical cards or materials) throughout your church's services, media, and programs?

- **Train staff in conversation skills.**

  Train greeters, small group leaders, and other people on the front lines of spiritual conversations in your church in healthy conversation and facilitation skills. Do they have what they need to be fully present, to maintain eye contact, to offer verbal and nonverbal cues as listeners, or to include people who might struggle to connect or speak up?

- **Encourage the congregation to develop their own stories.**

  Do individual Christians in your church know how to share their own story well? Perhaps a storytelling

or writing class at your church might focus on helping people uncover and communicate their own faith
background or personal experiences of God in a conversational, inviting way.

I realize that many of you reading this have some experience asking spiritual questions. But for those who struggle,
I hope you will give it a try. It takes getting outside your
comfort zone, opening yourself up to new experiences, and
having the courage to initiate with a stranger. None of these
things are easy! However, it is possible to have meaningful
spiritual conversations with people by asking spiritual discovery questions. These questions allow us to take an individual's past or current spiritual journey into consideration
and provide a space for them to share their ideas about the
afterlife without feeling pressure from us.

By taking time to listen thoughtfully and respond with
permission-based sharing, we can help our friends move
forward in their personal faith journeys, as well as draw
closer together in our understanding of one another. I say
"permission-based" because sharing requires consent. We
don't just want to ram our opinions down the throats of others. Instead, we want to engage with them respectfully. With
patience and prayerful discernment, these conversations can
open opportunities for further exploration of God's love and
grace that will bless both parties involved.

The Search
for Something More

A little more than twenty years ago, as the Harry Potter franchise was running full steam, I commissioned a project with Barna on "Teens and the Supernatural"—my second major Barna project with David Kinnaman as lead researcher. We were curious to know what teens believed about the supernatural, what they might have experimented with, and what they thought the Bible taught about these things.

While a significant number of teens had seen a Harry Potter movie or read one of the books, few reported that they had ever heard their pastor teach anything about the supernatural realm. This was surprising given that, at the time, there was a lot of Christian concern that Harry Potter was going to introduce the American population to witchcraft. That concern turned out to be largely unfounded. Twenty years later, our research shows that Harry Potter had little direct impact on the general population's spiritual identity, with only 12 percent reporting that they'd read a book about Wicca or witchcraft and only 6 percent having tried to cast a spell or mix a potion.

Fortune Tellers, Ghosts, and Other Mysteries

While certainly acknowledging that people have inherent spiritual curiosity, I wondered about the extent of their spiritual exploration. So as part of the research for this book, we asked individuals about their experiences with the supernatural and whether they would be receptive to exploring it further if invited by a friend.

Of the practices we asked about, the most often experienced supernatural activity among the spiritually curious is reading a horoscope, distantly followed by engaging a fortune teller or palm reader. Reading a book about witchcraft and using crystals was said to be experienced by only one in five spiritually curious people. (As a side note, Curious Skeptics were less likely than all U.S. adults to have explored half of the practices we asked about. They weren't significantly more likely than the Spiritually Curious to have participated in any with the exception of one.)

Now, just because the Spiritually Curious tried these things doesn't mean they actually had any faith in their effectiveness. Remember, the Spiritually Curious are driven by an inner curiosity that leads them to seek out new ideas and experiences that may help them gain insight into our strange universe. While not reported in large numbers, the Spiritually Curious are more likely than other groups to have

Horoscopes, Fortune-Telling Not Uncommon for the Spiritually Curious

Have you ever done any of the following? Select all that apply.

	All U.S. adults	Practicing Christians	Spiritually Curious	Curious Skeptics
Read or looked at your horoscope	51%	36%	55%	54%
Used a Ouija board	20%	13%	18%	26%
Witnessed a miracle	16%	26%	25%	9%
Had your fortune told	16%	14%	29%	14%
Had your palm read	16%	11%	27%	16%
Read a book about witchcraft or Wicca	12%	6%	20%	12%
Used crystals for healing properties	10%	5%	22%	15%
Played a game that featured witchcraft or psychic elements	9%	6%	12%	13%
Called or seen a psychic	9%	6%	15%	8%
Used mind-altering substances to have a spiritual or supernatural experience	8%	6%	15%	12%
Visited a medium or some other spiritual guide (not including a pastor, priest, or rabbi)	8%	5%	14%	5%
Tried to cast a spell or mix a magical potion	6%	3%	12%	5%
Participated in a séance	5%	2%	11%	5%
Been physically present when someone used psychic powers	5%	2%	11%	4%
Been physically present when someone performed a supernatural act	4%	4%	9%	4%
None of the above	27%	32%	17%	28%

n=1,501 U.S. adults, February 19–23, 2023. Source: Barna Group experimented with other occult-like phenomena—like visiting a medium, trying to cast a spell, and participating in a séance—showing their openness to exploration even if it's not widespread.

While I don't encourage anyone to experiment with these practices, it is helpful to have some understanding and awareness that allows for thoughtful engagement. Tarot, a popular form of fortune-telling, is an ancient system of divination that has been around since at least the fifteenth century. Horoscopes are a form of astrology that attempt to predict one's future through alignment of the stars and planets. Yoga is an ancient spiritual practice from India that combines physical postures, breathing techniques, and meditation to cultivate a deeper connection with one's spiritual self. While most yoga today is practiced more for its physical benefits than any sort of supernatural connection, it is important to note its ties for those exploring deeper levels of human spirituality. Many who practice yoga are probably aware of its spiritual roots, even if they don't see doing yoga as an explicitly spiritual practice in and of itself. I'll share more about mindfulness practices like yoga later.

Of course, not all spiritually curious people are experimenting with palm readers or fortune tellers. Our research tells us that people also connect with God through spending time in nature and journaling their thoughts (see Spiritually Open survey on p. 228). These practices are not as "exotic" as some of the others described in this chapter, but they stem from a similar desire to tap into something deeper.

Spiritually curious people are often drawn to spiritual exploration and practices like checking their horoscopes due to the potential insight these things may provide into their lives and the world around them. They may think of engaging in these practices more as spiritual research than an actual religious discipline. While not everyone believes in things like tarot, horoscopes, or palm reading, those who do are in pursuit of ways to better understand the mysterious realm of the supernatural and its connection to them.

Where Did All of This Begin?

Divination and fortune-telling appears in the Bible. But the spread of these practices in America gives us some interesting insights into our current cultural landscape.

The rise of spiritualism in America began around the time of the Civil War and has had a lasting influence on American culture. During the Civil War period, Americans were searching for answers to the tragedy and destruction caused by the war. Many turned to spiritualism as a way to make sense of their grief and come to terms with death. Spiritualists believed that it was possible to communicate with those who had passed away, as a means of providing comfort and solace during these difficult times. This practice of trying to communicate with the dead quickly became accepted, and the growing interest in spiritualism began to have a widespread impact on the nation.

Many embraced the ideas and practices associated with spiritualism in their daily lives, often mixing its practices with more traditional Christian beliefs and disciplines. Even President Abraham Lincoln was no stranger to spiritualism. Lincoln was nothing if not a curious man, and during his time in the White House, he held séances with his wife,

Mary Todd, in an attempt to contact their deceased son, Willie. They even invited guests to attend these séances, and there appeared to be no effort to conceal their existence or any concern that holding them would result in a political scandal. Clearly, even those in positions of power and influence had a deep and public interest in spiritualism during this era.

Part of the reason for this may be the relatively high prevalence of death during this era. It wasn't uncommon for a family to lose half of the children born into it during this time. Child mortality was incredibly high, and the front room, or parlor, would serve as the place where the coffin of a loved one would lay in wait before burial. Unlike today, death was not hidden from everyday life. It was easier to accept the idea that the dead might not be as far removed from the living as we think of them today.

The origin of the Ouija board dates back to the era that immediately followed the Civil War. It was created in the late 1880s by Charles Kennard, who was also a coffin maker. Ouija boards were originally called "talking boards." They use a planchette to spell out words and answer questions on an alphabet board. Players place their hands on the planchette in an attempt to communicate with spirits from beyond. For those open to spiritual phenomena, the Ouija board offered convenient access to explore the world beyond. The board became so popular it received a patent in 1890 and in one year during the 1960s outsold Monopoly as a popular game. The patent for the Ouija doesn't explain how it works, just that it does, and while people still claim it works, scientists have given reasons why they believe it does by perfectly natural means.[1]

As somewhat evidenced by these historical accounts and the Lincoln story, spiritualism has also been seen as a form of entertainment—like hiring a piano player for an event. In the mid to late 1800s, it wasn't unheard of for a medium to conduct a séance at a dinner party. These séances were often seen as the highlight of the evening, especially among high-society circles where people were eager to hear what their deceased loved ones had to say about the afterlife. For the May 1, 1920, issue of the *Saturday Evening Post*, Norman Rockwell painted a cover featuring a couple using a Ouija board. It wasn't until 1973, with the release of *The Exorcist*, that the Ouija became the taboo tool of the devil its often framed as today.[2]

Today's Spiritually Curious are little different than those from the past, continuing to explore and try to understand the supernatural world around them in an attempt to find meaning for today. Even today, spiritualism continues to be a part of American life, often mixing Christian beliefs with these practices. The data shows this through the number of people who feel comfortable exploring esoteric ideas while simultaneously holding Christian viewpoints, and vice versa.

Many of the esoteric spiritual practices popularized by the Spiritually Curious are seen as taboo or heretical in orthodox Christian circles though. The use of Ouija boards, tarot cards, horoscopes, and other forms of divination are widely considered to be dangerous or blasphemous. A spiritually curious person who opens up to a Christian about reading a horoscope or using a Ouija board may be met with terror, panic, or even anger. They may feel judged for their curiosity and decide that the Christian church is not a safe place for them.

Yet despite this disapproval, many people in the Christian faith are exploring these spiritual practices and believe they can find answers about an unknown future and life after death. Rather than be repulsed, condescending, or, worse, frightened by these things, what if we saw them as indicators of a person's search for meaning in the world? An activity that, while misguided, might be evidence of a soul that is desperately looking for a connection to the God of the universe that we know can be satisfied only through Jesus Christ? What if, instead of judging or condemning a person who talks about using tarot cards, we said, "I also believe in the supernatural realm and our ability as humans to connect to it. Can I tell you about some spiritual practices that have helped me?" Consider the following examples.

The Ancients Explored

The apostle Paul's sermon on Mars Hill was a remarkable example of the willingness of ancient people to explore spiritual matters. Paul stood before the Areopagus, an Athenian council known for its intellectual discourse and spiritual inquiries, and spoke about his faith in Jesus Christ. He urged the council members to search for a deeper understanding of God and discussed his belief in eternal life after death. Paul knew his audience had very different beliefs about the spiritual world than he had, but he also knew they had one thing in common: a belief in a spiritual realm and a hunger to know more about it. So he started there.

We can learn from Paul by first appreciating the spiritual curiosity in others when we learn about it. Rather than react negatively or in disgust, we can use that knowledge as a jumping-off point for deeper spiritual discussion.

An acquaintance once pulled out a Ouija board at a party I was attending. Because I'm known as a Christian minister in my community, people were intrigued to see my response. What was fascinating to me, as an observer of human spiritual searching, was the variety of responses at the party. Some were immediately concerned—even frightened. Others were excited. And still others felt awkward because they knew that I was in the room and weren't sure how to react in front of me. This was an Areopagus moment for me. How often are you at a party with a mix of people across the faith spectrum and the host opens the floor to discussions of a spiritual nature?

We have to be prepared for these kinds of encounters. We should also be so active in our communities that we find ourselves in these places as well. And we should make sure we live nonjudgmental lives, so people will feel free to raise these opportunities—trusting that we will not react poorly. If we aren't prepared for these things, how will others ever hear about Jesus?

As I mentioned earlier, it turns out there *is* something to the movement created by the Ouija board, and it has little to do with departed spirits. Rather, the science is in our minds: something described as ideomotor functions. It's a little tough to explain in a book, but if you ever meet me, ask me to give you a demonstration. I've freaked out more than a few people showing this phenomenon.

Oracles Explained

While the Ouija board is supposedly a tool to make contact with a departed spirit, or perhaps an evil spirit, tarot cards and other fortune-telling systems are oracles. An oracle is someone or something that people use to get advice and help them make decisions. For instance, in ancient times, people went to the Oracle of Delphi for answers. People also thought oracles could tell them things that would happen in the future. Kings and rulers used oracles to make important decisions regarding their country, often going into or avoiding war based on the insights that they received.

I am often surprised by the prevalence of tarot cards in people's lives. Bookstores and Kickstarter projects abound with different designs and styles, showing the tarot's role as a modern-day oracle. There are novelty tarot decks, where people can buy cards with Lord of the Rings or Star Trek themes. Sometimes people just like the designs. Sometimes people put real spiritual stock in their powers. Sometimes it's a little bit of both. Though tarot cards aren't now considered prophetic like their oracle predecessors in earlier cultures, the use of tarot cards is often believed to provide a person with clarity to move forward at times when they are feeling stuck, uncertain, or lost.

Saul's encounter with the Witch of Endor is an interesting story on this subject that is found in the Old Testament. In this story, Saul, the first king of Israel, has fallen out of favor with God. He goes to a witch in desperation, seeking insight into what his future holds.

Samuel the prophet had died some time before Saul sought the witch's guidance. Despite this, Saul believed that he could somehow communicate with Samuel through the witch. The Witch of Endor was able to conjure up a spirit in the form of Samuel and provide insight to Saul from beyond the grave. While biblical scholars debate whether Samuel really appeared or it was a deception created by the witch, the story shows how deeply entrenched spiritualism is in humanity's history and how desperate people can be in their search to know more.

This section of Scripture is one of the earliest recordings we have of someone specifically seeking help from sources outside the traditional religious structure. It would be a stretch to think of Saul as "Spiritually Curious," but he was doing something spiritually curious people do: experimenting with different spiritual practices outside the norm in a time of need. Similarly, the Spiritually Curious will often seek out advice from beyond the physical world too. While we as Christians have good reason to reject these tools, we can see them as potential indicators of the Spiritually Curious searching for answers to their questions. And we can have a voice in their search, if we have a good grasp on our beliefs and a genuine interest in their journey, hopes, dreams, fears, and questions.

The Search for Meaning

Although the majority of Americans believe in a supernatural realm, most tell us they haven't experienced something that could be explained only by supernatural or spiritual reasons. When we look by segment, we see that Naturalists and Curious Skeptics are far less likely than the Spiritually Curious and Practicing Christians to have had a spiritual experience.

This makes me think of the success the Alpha course has had in engaging groups. The U.K.—one of the more post-Christian Western countries in the world today—is where Alpha was birthed. It's a little hard to describe what Alpha is. The Alpha course is a transformative program that offers individuals an opportunity to explore the foundations of

More Than Half of Spiritually Curious Have Had a Supernatural Experience

Have you ever personally experienced something that could only be explained by supernatural or spiritual reasons?

	All U.S. adults	Practicing Christians	Spiritually Curious	Curious Skeptics	Naturalists
Yes	39%	47%	63%	29%	16%
No	61%	53%	37%	71%	84%

n=1,501 U.S. adults, February 19–23, 2023. Source: Barna Group

Christianity in a thought-provoking and engaging manner, providing a space for participants to ask questions, delve into meaningful discussions, and develop a deeper understanding of their faith journey. It isn't a Bible study, per se. But it is about Christianity and trusting Jesus. The course takes place as a weekly meal and discussion over eleven weeks. The conclusion of the program is a weekend retreat where people are given time to reflect on the course and encouraged to take some time to let God speak. The testimonies of what people encounter and experience in that last meeting together are amazing.

While we don't need an intellectual reason or miraculous intervention to have a vibrant faith in God, an experience like this is exactly what many are looking for. People who are actively experimenting with their spirituality are exactly who we need to introduce to Jesus.

Let's take a look at what our research turned up on American's beliefs about what happens after death, so we can better appreciate their search for meaning in times of uncertainty. Given the wide variance in people's beliefs, we summarized the most frequent responses and asked respondents to answer what most closely reflected their beliefs.

I've mentioned several times that our research shows people are complicated when it comes to their spirituality, and the data from the chart on page 67 confirms that. Consider the Practicing Christian who believes in reincarnation or the Naturalist (defined by the fact that they believe the natural world is all there is) believing there is judgment by God for the choices made on earth. People's spiritual beliefs aren't easily categorized into traditional boxes and labels. Many people have deeply nuanced, thoughtful reasons for why they believe two things that, at first glance, seem to be contradictory. It doesn't always add up, but then again, this provides confidence for us that engaging the Spiritually Curious is important. It's only by really talking to people that percentages take on human dimension.

What is significant is that nearly half of the U.S. population and 39 percent of the Spiritually Curious believe people are accountable in a cosmic way for how they live on earth. In short, roughly one in two people in America believe that some sort of divine reckoning is coming. That is soil for the gospel seed to germinate and bear fruit.

We also looked at the life-after-death question another way, asking what people believed would happen to them personally after they died. Forty-two percent of the total population aren't sure what will happen when they die, including 38 percent of the Spiritually Curious (see the chart on p. 129).

While you may be troubled to see that only 59 percent of Practicing Christians believe they will go to heaven through

Half of Spiritually Curious Have a Traditional View of God

There are many different beliefs about God or a higher power. Please choose which one of the following descriptions comes closest to what you, personally, believe about God.

	All U.S. adults	Practicing Christians	Spiritually Curious	Curious Skeptics	Naturalists
God is the all-powerful, all-knowing, perfect Creator of the universe who rules the world today	49%	87%	50%	32%	5%
God represents a state of higher consciousness that a person may reach	15%	5%	13%	18%	14%
There is no such thing as God	12%	–	3%	19%	65%
God refers to the total realization of personal, human potential	10%	2%	7%	15%	7%
Everyone is god	7%	5%	14%	6%	5%

n=1,501 U.S. adults, February 19–23, 2023. Source: Barna Group

confession of sins and accepting Christ, we need to remember that all Christians who are in this category have professed these things. These are Christians who say they have confessed their sins to God and have trusted Jesus for their salvation. Still, in this question, they do not believe those are the criteria that get them into heaven. Based on this, we have many Christians in our churches who attend regularly, read their Bible, and pray, and still either remain skeptical of orthodox Christian teachings, struggle to grasp them, or perhaps simply haven't had them fully explained yet.

How do these groups see God?

Only Naturalists are likely to be true atheists, with about half of the total U.S. adult population adhering to the traditional Judeo-Christian view of God. In an era of open spirituality, it's crucial to clarify what we mean by "God," and also what those we are speaking to mean by that word. People who are Spiritually Curious are often keen to share and learn about different beliefs regarding God. A compelling way to engage them is to ask how they arrived at their current beliefs about God. Many of these individuals have formed opinions about God somewhat unconsciously. Many times the question helps them realize how vague what they assume they know really is. In discussions, I find spiritually curious people are generally intrigued by the idea of

The Curious Are Content without Answers

Among the following, which would you say best describes your spiritual beliefs today?

	All U.S. adults	Practicing Christians	Spiritually Curious	Curious Skeptics	Naturalists
I feel comfortable and certain about my beliefs	36%	50%	38%	30%	23%
I feel content that I don't have all the answers	33%	17%	26%	40%	46%
I feel compelled to dig deeper and learn more about what I believe	21%	30%	30%	17%	11%
I feel unsure about who to trust or what to believe	10%	4%	6%	14%	20%

n=1,501 U.S. adults, February 19–23, 2023. Source: Barna Group

a relatable God. While some people are steadfast in their beliefs, there are others who have less confidence in what they believe at any given moment. So we asked about that too.

The Curious Skeptics seem generally okay with their ambiguity, which plays to their posture of being both curious and skeptical. But we can all see there is an intellectual humility among many of the profiles, which certainly implies a willingness to learn more. This is also true among many Practicing Christians, many of whom express confidence and certainty in what they believe, while 30 percent desire to learn more about their beliefs. Overall, we see that many people are open to the idea that there is more to learn about their spiritual beliefs.

Mindfulness

The last several years have seen an increase in the science of spirituality. Christian spirituality experts and secular seekers of spiritual truth alike have gained many insights from the work being done in the field of neuroscience. This is helping us better understand the idea of holistic wellness, or "mindfulness," from a neurological perspective.

For Christians, this should not be surprising. Science is one of the tools God gave us to better understand both the world around us and ourselves. It stands to reason that this tool would be effective. After all, if God created the hardware, he also provides the software for getting the most out of life. This software is what we might call "open source"—it can be used by anyone, regardless of whether they worship the One who designed it. For example, a friend of mine who would call himself a "neo-pagan" describes his spiritual practices as being deity-free, hacking the bio-spiritual reality that exists in each of us.

And you can find versions of some Christian disciplines in common wellness practices. Your church worship music is not so dissimilar from Eastern yoga practices of meditation with chanting, repeating, and controlled breathing that creates euphoric experiences. These things have been a

The Curious Embrace Meditation & Mindfulness

Do you . . . ? Select all that apply.

	All U.S. adults	Practicing Christians	Spiritually Curious	Curious Skeptics	Naturalists
Meditate	31%	37%	47%	34%	11%
Practice mindfulness	24%	22%	35%	25%	13%
Use herbal supplements	22%	22%	34%	22%	18%
Practice yoga	17%	13%	32%	19%	11%
Use psychedelics	6%	2%	17%	10%	7%
Practice homeopathy	6%	5%	14%	7%	5%
Seek to enhance sexual experience through practices like Tantric sex or Kama Sutra	5%	4%	10%	7%	1%

n=1,501 U.S. adults, February 19–23, 2023. Source: Barna Group

great help for some people dealing with things like stress and anxiety. But is this really the experience of God?

In Ecclesiastes, the author Qoheleth searches for meaning under the sun (here on earth apart from God) and finds many satisfying experiences. Yet in the end, he concludes that all is vanity of vanities, a vapor, a meaningless chasing of the wind. Just because something "worked" didn't mean it provided him with meaning or purpose.

Our modern understanding of our fantastic bodies and minds may indeed lead us to create spiritual hacks that Qoheleth didn't access, but his report would be the same today as it was at the time he assembled the data in Ecclesiastes. Many wellness disciplines may have practical uses for our bodies and our minds. But knowing God, and connecting to him—the one who is greater than all that is under the sun—is unique beyond what is materially created.

How do we tangibly experience this relationship with God? How do we help others experience this?

The chart on page 161 shows some current practices in what we'll broadly call "the wellness movement"—the quest for physical, mental, emotional, and spiritual well-being. The Spiritually Curious are more likely than Practicing Christians to engage in these practices.

In light of the mindfulness trends, how can the church reimagine itself?

The Well

Aaron Bjerke pastors The Well in New York City, a church plant out of Redeemer Presbyterian where he worked as an assistant pastor under Tim Keller. The Well is the most intentional effort I've seen to embrace the Spiritually Curious with an entirely different approach to church.

"Throughout my pastoral experience over the past decade, I've noticed a new demographic emerging through questions that I've been asked by other congregants," Aaron explained. "There is a growing sub-demographic in the secular population that is searching for a spiritual experience, and it hasn't received a lot of attention from the church. Whether it's feeling stressed at work, increasingly dissatisfied with a relationship or money, postmodern Americans are increasingly seeking a spiritual remedy."[3]

Meditation rooms are the hottest new work perk, with many offices now offering quiet places for employees to retreat for a few minutes and decompress. CEOs are personally seeking out a practice of meditation to become better leaders. One observation is that the meditation movement is where the yoga movement was in the mid-1990s, which means the ceiling for the market is still miles high. Don't be surprised if you start seeing meditation become even bigger in the coming years. Don't be terrified either.

Meditation looks like a lot of different things for different people. The market represents a spectrum of practices—such as mindfulness, Transcendental Meditation, or various forms of Buddhism—and promises an experience of peace, productivity, happiness, and so on. This is done by taking back control of the mind and taming it. At its simplest and most secular, meditation is simply taking a few minutes to quiet the chatter in your brain and smooth out some of the tensions. But different strains of meditation may layer in various spiritual elements.

Consumers of these practices are generally not skeptics—the Richard Dawkinses of the world who are hostile toward spirituality—nor are they necessarily seekers who are exploring the Christian faith and dialoguing with Christians (although they might be!). Those two groups have been engaged with success through various evangelism programs. Rather, those in the meditation market are what I'm calling *searchers*: seculars searching for a spiritual experience. Meditation can function as a sort of religious practice for people who do not consider themselves religious. Remember that most people are drawn toward the spiritual world, regardless of whether they're aware of it. Meditation is one way many people explore this natural pull in a safe, low-stakes environment.

You can see why Aaron Bjerke and I instantly hit it off. He was living out as a pastor everything I was observing in my travels and research.

I'm not sure whether The Well is a church or the ultimate "church spa" experience! I asked Aaron to describe what it was like to attend a service at The Well.

> Services are a place of serenity, care, and rest. Both Christians and the spiritual but not religious have felt a deep sense of peace when they step into our auditorium. We create a serene and peaceful atmosphere with our lo-fi beats music, setting the stage for a truly immersive experience.
>
> Our service begins with a captivating 90-second video featuring calligraphy that relates to the current season of the church calendar. This is followed by a welcoming introduction that speaks directly to the non-religious, ensuring that everyone feels included and understood. We then move into two songs, presented through our unique lo-fi beats lens. We believe in the power of beauty, using art to create a healing environment that touches the soul.

Our sermon is purposefully designed to be 20 minutes long, similar to a TED Talk. We've received rave reviews from our non-religious attendees, who have likened it to a "TED Talk on marriage." We value coherence and respect for our audience's time, providing a concise and impactful message. After the sermon, we invite you to join us in a guided meditation for 10 minutes. This is a truly transformative experience that allows space for personal reflection and connection with the Divine.

At The Well, we strive to create a humble and inclusive church service. We break the mold by sitting in silence after the sermon and offering a guided meditation. This moment of stillness and listening is the most spirit-led and accessible part of our service. We believe that everyone can benefit from this experience, regardless of their familiarity with Scripture or religious practices.

To conclude our service, we partake in communion, a sacramental and deeply significant moment. This is not just a symbolic act of remembrance, but a powerful and tangible encounter with the divine.[4]

COVID disrupted the growth trajectory of The Well, but I'm excited to see Aaron and the community building again. And I look forward to seeing how God uses this fascinating church experience to be introduced to the Spiritually Curious.

As we meet the Spiritually Curious, we will probably encounter many people who have experimented with meditation, horoscopes, tarot cards, and other spiritual practices. While Christians may be skeptical of these things and reject their usefulness, we should be careful to not reject the *people* who use these things. They are, after all, engaging in their curiosity about the spiritual world with whatever tools they have on hand. We can encourage this curiosity by asking questions, remembering that the search for truth and meaning may take a few detours on the way to the ultimate Source of all truth and meaning. Some Christians have acted as guard dogs who growl threateningly at people who get off the right path, sometimes scaring those people from continuing their journey. But with God's help, we can act more as guides, helpfully pointing them back to truth in Jesus.

On Earth as
It Is in Heaven

My wife and I were staying with our friends in Orlando and were excited to take our son to the Magic Kingdom for the very first time. We woke up a little earlier than normal to get there first thing.

Dax, who was only three at the time, was up before us and playing with their son with some Happy Meal toys. It was time to load up the car, and Dax had decided he did not want to go with us. "But, Dax, we are going to ride rides and even see Mickey Mouse!"

He was not impressed. "I don't want to go to Disney World. I want to stay here."

When our efforts failed to convince him how wonderful the Magic Kingdom would be, I picked him up while he kicked, screaming and crying, and forced him into his car seat.

"You're going to Disney World and you're going to LOVE IT!" I said loudly, in an angry voice.

"But I don't want to go to Disney World. I don't want to go," he kept screaming.

This was not the scene I'd imagined from all the commercials I'd seen.

Heaven Is a Place on Earth

Reflecting on that moment, I've come to realize that this isn't completely unlike the problem we have convincing others of the promise of heaven and salvation that comes through Jesus.

Some people just don't want to go.

As C. S. Lewis said, "We are . . . like an ignorant child who wants to go on making mud pies in a slum because he cannot imagine what is meant by the offer of a holiday at the sea."[1]

I remember at our PlanetWisdom student conferences doing a teaching segment on what heaven would be like. MercyMe traveled with me in those days and had written "I Can Only Imagine" as a complement to the weekend's teaching.

I started getting letters about heaven and eternity from teenagers. (I'm dating myself, but back then, teenagers wrote letters!) What I read surprised me. Many Christian teenagers didn't want to go to heaven. To be clear, they definitely didn't want to go to hell. But in their minds, heaven didn't sound all that great either. They asked if God might be willing to just "extinguish" them, so they weren't in hell or heaven for eternity. If it were one obscure letter, I might have dismissed it. But I received around a dozen letters from teens across the country expressing the same thing. If heaven *was* real, they didn't want to go.

Houston, we have a heaven problem. What's going on? Then it hit me. Many teenagers have a poor understanding of heaven that has been derived from how we communicate the Christian faith. They imagine that we'll be on clouds playing harps all day.

Think about it. If you believed that heaven was going to be like a never-ending church service, twenty-four hours a day, seven days a week, *for the rest of time*, would you want to go? I wouldn't, and I'm part of planning our Sunday services! Sometimes, I wonder if even Jesus would want to go. Maybe, deep down, you've felt this way too. There's no shame in admitting it. Heaven, as we've come to explain it, doesn't sound particularly appealing.

The reality is that we see through a glass dimly and have done a poor job living on earth as it is in heaven. Most people simply have no context for what it would be like to spend eternity with God. So—to better engage the curious—we have to get in touch with what heaven is *really* like.

David John Seel shared it with me this way:

The gospel has to be expanded to be beyond redemption—from a fall and redemption to creation, fall, redemption, *and* restoration, which basically means the purpose of the gospel is the renewal of all of life in the here and now. And to enter into kingdom vitality right here and now. There'll be no more resources in heaven that are not presently available now. And the challenge of the church is to get heaven into us, not simply to get us into heaven. And that actually, heaven is the environment in which we live, and the creation and the kingdom of God is right here, right now. And when we talk about the gospel, the gospel is not cross-centered, it is resurrection-centered. Jesus talked about how the kingdom of heaven is at hand, which basically means resurrection life available to you right now, to enable you to be fully the person you can be and only can be when you're connected to the reality in which you are designed to flourish.[2]

The offer of Christ isn't to bounce around on the clouds for all time. It is the ability to experience heaven on earth now! Our eschatology may have created an urgency to evangelize the world, but by failing to teach the entire story of the Good News, it's tainted our message here on earth.

For many spiritually curious people, the idea that becoming a Christian is all about going to heaven when you die makes our current lives here feel dull and meaningless. After all, why should we create art or care for the environment when it's all going to burn anyway? If becoming a Christian is just an escape ladder, then why should anyone bother sticking around?

But true Christian teaching isn't just about what happens when we die—it means our eternal life begins in the here and now! Our motto should be, "We polish brass on sinking ships!" Why? Because that is the extravagance of the kingdom. That is the hope of the gospel. We are always co-creators with God making all things new. The problem is that we aren't "making" much of anything these days other than big buildings with large asphalt moats surrounding them. That is the "eternal life" being modeled for the watching world. Why would anyone want to spend an eternity doing this?

Randy Alcorn, author and founder of the nonprofit Eternal Perspective Ministries, has written, "The best of life on Earth is a glimpse of Heaven; the worst of life is a glimpse of Hell. For Christians, this present life is the closest they will come to Hell. For nonbelievers, it is the closest they will come to Heaven."[3]

If Alcorn's quote is true, then we need to start living heaven out on earth. It may be the greatest testimony we have—that Christians have a picture of an ideal for humankind, and we have been given spiritual power to make it known right now!

The good news here is that most people do believe in some sort of heaven. While not as confident as Practicing Christians, 80 percent of the Spiritually Curious believe heaven is a real place. In other words, the hard work of convincing most people that there is some sort of heaven has already been accomplished. The real work is convincing them what it might look like.

The best way to do that isn't by casting more visions of white robes, golden halos, and harp-playing marathons. It's by living lives that speak to the power of heaven in the here and now. And that reality is embedded in the Lord's Prayer: "Thy kingdom come, Thy will be done in earth, as it is in heaven" (Matt. 6:10 KJV).

If heaven is the ideal place, and it is part of our future experience, that explains why Christians should be marked by future thinking and progress. In fact, this used to be the case. In his book *The Victory of Reason: How Christianity Led to Freedom, Capitalism, and Western Success*,

Most of the Spiritually Curious Say Heaven Is Real

Please indicate how certain you are that heaven is a real place.

	All U.S. adults	Practicing Christians	Spiritually Curious	Curious Skeptics	Naturalists
Completely certain	44%	83%	50%	24%	1%
Somewhat certain	23%	11%	29%	29%	4%
Somewhat not certain	15%	3%	10%	21%	24%
Not at all certain	18%	3%	10%	26%	70%

n=1,501 U.S. adults, February 19–23, 2023. Source: Barna Group

sociologist of religion Rodney Stark wrote that in the early church "Christianity was oriented to the future, while the other major religions asserted the superiority of the past. At least in principle, if not always in fact, Christian doctrines could always be modified in the name of progress as demonstrated by reason."[4]

To better understand heaven will require us to more richly understand Scripture and wrestle with both our own sin and the way it manifests in our city and neighborhoods on a systemic level. It will also challenge us to come up with more creative ways to address that sin proactively, working together to build communities that reflect the kingdom of God. The process of creating and making is a transforming experience. When we come together as a church to live heaven on earth, this will deepen our own soul and our own relationship with Jesus. And rather than heaven being seen as a 24/7 church service, it will be seen as a whole new way of being.

In case it wasn't clear, this isn't something any of us can do alone. As pastor and author Andy Crouch writes in *Culture Making: Recovering Our Creative Calling*,

> So do you want to make culture? Find a community, a small group who can lovingly fuel your dreams and puncture your illusions. Find friends and form a family who are willing to see grace at work in one another's lives, who can discern together which gifts and which crosses each has been called to bear. Find people who have a holy respect for power and a holy willingness to spend their power alongside the powerless. Find some partners in the wild and wonderful world beyond church doors. And then, together, make something of the world.[5]

To do this well, we need to get out of our comfort zones and start working and creating at the full capacity of who God created us to be. We need to find our flow.

Finding Our Flow

Renowned psychologist Mihaly Csikszentmihalyi discovered and defined a state of optimum performance he called *flow*. He described it this way: "The best moments in our lives are not the passive, receptive, relaxing times. . . . The best moments usually occur if a person's body or mind is stretched to its limits in a voluntary effort to accomplish something difficult and worthwhile."[6]

You've probably felt flow at different times in your life. Maybe you called it being "in the zone" or having a "creative breakthrough." Whatever it is, it's a good feeling. It's what happens when time disappears and we experience optimal focus and achievement. I've experienced it several times just writing this book. I wake up, start writing, and in what seems like minutes, my wife is calling me for dinner. Where did the time go? It was a eudaemonistic experience of finding deep satisfaction, meaning, and purpose as I strove to do my best work.

But realistically, those times weren't even peak flow experience, because I was alone in front of my computer when I had them. Studies show that flow is better experienced when working with others. Students rated flow to be more enjoyable when in a team rather than when they were alone. Students also found it more joyful if the team members were able to talk to one another. This finding was replicated even when skill level and challenge were equal.[7]

So, how do we do it? How do we find our flow? Well, there are at least as many ways as there are people in the world. To get into flow you need to find a challenging activity that stretches your skill to complete it. Too easy and you get bored. Too challenging for your skill level and you will be frustrated. A good first step is to find something that brings you a lot of joy but also a little intimidation.

Many of us find flow in our hobbies—the kind of work we do even though there may not be an economic reason for doing it. It may be a creative pursuit, a physical challenge, or a volunteer effort in the community. The kind of work you would do for free if you could. Some experience the joy of vocations that do this, but many do not.

When I think of the experience of heaven on earth, I think about this experience of flow. I think heaven is a group of people working together, in community, to worship God in an uncountable variety of ways we can hardly even imagine now. I don't know if there are "days" in heaven, but if there are, I don't think any two of them will be the same. I think heaven will be challenging and that we will have opportunities to stretch and grow in our skill. I believe this because that is what I want now all the time. And we can offer these kinds of experiences to others right now.

This is why I think we need to be very careful about making church or the pursuit of spirituality "easier." It's not particularly helpful, nor is it even what most spiritually curious people are looking for. The Christian life can be demanding, and there is no reason for us to pretend otherwise. We want it to be challenging, while still working to tailor the experience for where people are currently in their pilgrimage. When we do this right, we're encouraging people to find a spiritual flow state—"wrestling" experiences that are transformational. If spiritually curious people enjoy challenging activities— even paying for such experiences on vacation and with their extracurricular time—why wouldn't we offer similar experiences in our churches as well?

A Glimpse of Heaven

One of the ways we can show a glimpse of heaven to others is by doing something so overwhelmingly excellent for them that it defies any standard by which they have been treated. Extraordinary acts of kindness or unexpected generosity (particularly from strangers) blow people's minds.

Extraordinary generosity also tends to be contagious. Barna's research for *The State of Generosity* shows that those who give have been given to. Specifically, more than half of U.S. adults who have given charitably within the year (54 percent) say that at some point in their life they have been the recipient of someone else's extraordinary generosity (as opposed to 36 percent of those who are not donors).[8] Great kindness can be arresting. In the face of it, people might encounter a turning point or be changed for the better.

The movement known as Tips for Jesus began in 2013 when an anonymous person started leaving generous tips at restaurants and bars with the hashtag #TipsForJesus. While Christians aren't typically known for their extravagant gratuity (ask someone in the service industry about their Sunday church crowd experience), a mystery person started leaving hundreds or even thousands of dollars on the table, all in the name of Jesus. One inspiring story is of a server in Oregon who received a $1,000 tip, which she used to buy a car and take her family on a much-needed vacation. Over time, more people began participating, with some leaving tips as high as $10,000.

The social media account soon grew to nearly seventy-five thousand followers, and people began speculating about who was behind it.

Eventually, the mystery was revealed: the extravagant tipper was former PayPal vice president Jack Selby. He explained that #TipsForJesus wasn't originally intended to be an explicitly Christian movement. He just thought it was the sort of thing Jesus would do. "The name encapsulated the spirit of giving," he later told the dining website Eater. "So we went with it."[9] Restaurant workers, many of whom work long hours for low pay, were receiving life-changing amounts of money, all connected to Jesus.

If you seek to live a kingdom-pursuing life, there is no doubt that you have at some point caught the attention of a spiritually curious person. These are some of the most exciting moments as a Christian, when people see you doing something they can't figure out.

"Why are you doing this?" they ask, their natural curiosity piqued by a display of extravagant generosity, kindness, or empathy. And the only reason you can possibly give is the hope you have in following in the way of Jesus.

Engaging the Curious

In pursuing heaven on earth, there are four biblical principles we can act on that inform how we can engage the Spiritually Curious.

Living on Earth as It Is in Heaven

In his book *Heaven: A Comprehensive Guide to Everything the Bible Says about Our Eternal Home*, Randy Alcorn writes that "if you read history, you will find that the Christians who did most for the present world were just those who thought most of the next."[10] This ought to shape how we as Christians think about heaven. It's not an excuse to sit on our heels and wait for an eventual happy ending. It's a motivation to bring our world ever more in line with the one yet to come. I recently served as the interim CEO of MOVEMENT.ORG, an organization that brings together the leaders in a city to ask, "What needs to move closer to God's design for human flourishing?"

How would you answer that for your city or neighborhood? What currently is falling short? With the Holy Spirit empowering all that is within us, why shouldn't we strive to live out the prayer Jesus taught us: to live life on earth as it is in heaven?

Heaven certainly doesn't resemble a boring Bible study or lifeless worship. The more we connect with the place where we are going and desire to bring it to earth, the more we will connect with the Spiritually Curious.

Making Things New

In 2005, a young NBA player named LeBron James was starting to attract some major attention. He'd single-handedly made the Cleveland Cavaliers a formidable presence in the NBA, and his performance was exceeding the enormous expectations he'd been saddled with. It wasn't long before people started whispering that he might be the real deal: the next Michael Jordan. The whispers grew loud enough that a journalist asked James point-blank how he felt about the comparison. "I don't want to be the next Michael Jordan," James replied. "I want to be LeBron James."[11]

There's a real lesson here for the rest of us. For Christians, the past is a useful teacher and a helpful guide. But God is a Creator, and he is in the business of creating new things. Revelation 21:5 says, "He who was seated on the throne said, 'I am making everything new!'"

This is the work Jesus is doing, and will do, with the old earth. He will make it new. New air, new trees, new dirt. I don't know about you, but I love new things. The Spiritually Curious are looking for new things too. Andy Crouch frames this well:

I wonder what we Christians are known for in the world outside our churches. Are we known as critics, consumers, copiers, condemners of culture? I'm afraid so. Why aren't we known as cultivators—people who tend and nourish what is best in human culture, who do the hard and painstaking work to preserve the best of what people before us have done? Why aren't we known as creators—people who dare to think and do something that has never been thought or done before, something that makes the world more welcoming and thrilling and beautiful?[12]

How is our spiritual community making things new for the neighbors around us? People get drawn into this kind of activity. I don't want to preserve something that is dead or dying; I want to bring life! I don't want to keep trying to pour old wine into old wineskins. I want to build something better. As Jesus said in John 10:10b, "I have come that they may have life, and have it to the full."

Seeking the Peace of Our City

The book of Jeremiah finds Judah, the southern kingdom of Israel, at a harrowing point in its history. It had just taken a beating from the Babylonians, as Babylon overpowered Jerusalem and took the people into captivity. Wars and battles are not pretty in any era, and they were particularly brutal in Jeremiah's day. Many soldiers had died painful deaths, and the survivors faced a life of exile and slavery.

Picture bandaging your wounds while comforting your distressed family as chaos has broken out and disrupted everything you have cherished in life. Young men and women are being snatched up to be put into servitude in a foreign land. You are the losers in battle and now the victors will reign over you.

It is into this scene that Jeremiah comes with a word from the Lord: "Also, seek the peace and prosperity of the city to which I have carried you into exile. Pray to the LORD for it, because if it prospers, you too will prosper" (29:7).

It's difficult for me to imagine how the people that this message was given to felt about these sentences. I think about Daniel, Hananiah, Mishael, and Azariah (the last three we know better by their Babylonian names: Shadrach, Meshach, and Abednego). They were all taken away from their homes to serve in Babylon. Yet, amidst this national punishment that had come about because the people were not following the Lord, they brilliantly walked the line of humbly serving their captors while never disobeying or turning their backs on God. The Bible records amazing accounts of remarkable moments when they showed deep trust in God while in exile. When their prescribed Babylonian diet went against Jewish law, they neither pitched a fit nor willingly obeyed. Instead, they proposed a simple test: asking their captors to let them continue eating a vegetarian diet for a few days to see if they looked any less healthy than the others. After ten days, the Babylonians had to admit that Daniel and his friends looked even healthier than they did (Dan. 1:3–16). Through this mix of patience, thoughtfulness, and conversation, Daniel, Hananiah, Mishael, and Azariah were able to both earn the freedom to maintain their religious practice and win the respect of others around them.

What might this look like for us today? We may not be living in captivity, but we know that our Christian way of life doesn't always run in perfect harmony with the world around us. We can bend over backward and submit to laws that go against our Christian principles, or we can stubbornly refuse to even associate with the rest of our community. Or we can be like Daniel and his friends, honoring God while seeking the peace of our cities, even when it requires a good deal of nuance.

Daniel, known "to have a keen mind and knowledge and understanding" (Dan. 5:12) as well as "wisdom and tact" (2:14), became "ruler over the entire province of Babylon and . . . in charge of all its wise men" (2:48). Years later, "he was proclaimed the third highest ruler in the kingdom" (5:29) and "the king planned to set him over the whole kingdom" (6:3). These incredibly important positions in the government show that Daniel devoted his life to the success of the kingdom where he lived as an exile, with deviations in his loyalty only when, as his enemies said, "it has something to do with the law of his God" (6:5).

I believe that if we can learn to live more like this in our present day, we can reach more spiritually curious people through a living testament to God's goodness and awesomeness.

Pursuing the Kingdom to Awaken the Image of God in People

If you are a Gen Xer or older, you've most likely heard of the iconic magician Doug Henning. His Broadway musical *The Magic Show*, television specials, and touring performances made him one of the best-known magicians of the 1970s. As a kid, I was intrigued by magicians—or *illusionists*, as we called them in my conservative Christian home. Making people appear and disappear, supposedly cutting people in two pieces then putting them together again, and all other kinds of wonderful things fascinated me. I was able to see Doug Henning live at the Pantages in California when I was a teenager, and when *Spellbound*, a book about Doug's life came out, I read a story that reminded me of what our purpose is as Christians. In 1971, Doug Henning traveled to a remote region near the North Pole where he performed magic for the Inuit people.

> They sat on the floor in their parkas, and I did what I thought was some pretty good stuff. They just sat there, didn't smile, didn't say a word and, at the end, nobody applauded. But they were completely focused on me, like I was some sort of phenomenon. Only one of them spoke English, so I asked him, "Did you like the show?"
>
> "Yes, we like the show," he said.
>
> Then I asked, "Did everyone like the magic?"
>
> He said, "The magic?"
>
> I explained that I was trying to entertain people.
>
> He said, "Entertainment is good, but why are you doing magic? The whole world is magical . . ."
>
> We sat down on the floor and he told me, "It's magic that the snow falls, all those little crystals are completely different . . . that's magic."
>
> Now I was gasping, trying to explain magic to him. I thought of my "Zombie," which I thought was my best thing. I said, "I made that beautiful silver ball float in the air. . . . That's magic."
>
> Then the Inuits started talking among themselves. The man came to me with a big smile on his face, and said, "Now, we know why you're doing that. It's because your people

have forgotten the magic. You're doing it to remind them of magic. Well done!"

I cried right then . . . I said, "Thank you for teaching me about the magic. I didn't know." That was really the first time I knew what wonder was. It was the most memorable thing that has ever happened to me. I never forgot that, inside. That's why I became a magician.[13]

Many of us who are followers of Jesus are like Doug Henning. Just like he'd lost touch with wonder, replacing it with party tricks and Broadway theatrics, we've forgotten what is truly amazing about the power of the gospel. So much of what we must do today is to *remember* the power of the gospel, the awesomeness of grace. In the third chapter of Ecclesiastes, Qoheleth writes, "He has also set eternity in the human heart; yet no one can fathom what God has done from beginning to end" (3:11).

Somehow, we as Christians have failed to envision the glory of heaven—the magical wonderfulness of it. We've stopped short of pursuing the kingdom in our cities and neighborhoods. The world has neglected the shard of the imago Dei in humanity, broken by sin, that wants so desperately to reflect the image of God. Maybe part of the reason the world is losing touch with it is that we Christians, who are in the best position to connect people to that shard, are failing them.

"Why Are Christians So Boring?"

Our family likes to go to museums, attend live concerts, and enjoy the theater. We accidentally stumbled on David Byrne's

American Utopia on one of our visits to see our kids in New York City. The experience was so amazing, we went twice. While walking out of the show, deeply affected, I asked my family, "Why are Christians so boring?"

My adult children and I have lamented about this all their lives. We'd attend a live concert by one of their favorite indie bands and they'd ask, "Why is this so much more fun than worship on Sunday morning?" I didn't know how to answer, other than that I'm pretty sure the concert we just attended wouldn't feel the same on a Sunday morning either!

My indictment of Christianity isn't meant to be an attack. After all, I'm a Christian. I'm criticizing myself too! The simple fact of the matter is that we rarely clock in at the top of our fields, particularly in the arts. While there are certainly many passionate, skilled Christian artists who are doing beautiful work, it's safe to say that very few of the most notable artists of our day come from the church. Why might this be? After all, as we've seen, most people in America identify as Christians. Why are so few of us represented among the most compelling and celebrated creative fields of our time?

As it turns out, there has been some research done on why this might be the case. Researcher Dana R. Carney wrote, "We obtained consistent and converging evidence that personality differences between liberals and conservatives are robust, replicable, and behaviorally significant, especially with respect to social (vs. economic) dimensions of ideology. In general, liberals are more open-minded, creative, curious, and novelty seeking, whereas conservatives are more orderly, conventional, and better organized."[14]

Obviously, not every American Christian is politically or socially conservative. However, Christians in America do statistically tend to lean conservative, which means Carney's research may contain at least part of the answer to our question. But does that alone sentence the conservative-leaning Christian to a life devoid of artistic creativity and imagination? Stephen Dollinger, researcher at Southern Illinois University, went a little further in the introduction to his paper "Creativity and Conservatism" with a survey overview of the issue:

> [Glenn] Wilson theorized conservatism as based on a generalized fear of uncertainty. However, it can be viewed more broadly as "motivated social cognition" driven by epistemic, existential, and ideological motivations with two core aspects—fear of change and tolerance of inequality (Jost, Glaser, Kruglanski & Sulloway, 2003a). Given Wilson's theory, there are at least three reasons to expect less creativity among conservatives.
>
> First, individuals who are threatened by uncertainty may be disposed to focus on lower-order needs to increase their safety and security (e.g., Bar-Tal, 2001, Maslow, 1987). This focus is inconsistent with the motivations that prompt creativity. Second, conformity to what is conventionally accepted focuses the individual on traditions (what is old), whereas all definitions of creativity include a focus on what is new (Mayer, 1999). As Runco (2004) noted, creativity not only responds to current problems or challenges but is "one of the engines of cultural evolution" (p. 658). This association with societal change may provoke anxiety in conservatives. Third, the authoritarian and anti-hedonistic elements of the construct would lead conservatives to devalue imagination.[15]

This may come across as a bit harsh or pejorative. However, our research for this book is consistent with many of these points, and it does ring true. Earlier, we talked about the higher need for closure and lower curiosity scores reported by Practicing Christians as being less true in the Spiritually Curious. Churches with largely conservative populations are statistically less likely to have people drawn to creativity.

I bring this up not to insult conservatives (I am one!) but to help us understand that we come from a cognitive culture that struggles to appeal to the curious. Those who are spiritually curious are not likely to feel at home in many of our churches, because so much of church culture is built and maintained by people who fundamentally think differently than they do. We Christians are much better suited to debate the staunch atheist than we are to create a meaningful experience of spiritual discovery for those looking to encounter God differently or, in some cases, accurately.

It's important to note, though, that our churches have many believers who also score high in their curiosity and with less than a high need for closure. These naturally curious Christians are likely starving for a satisfying spiritual experience in church, attending Sunday after Sunday, wondering why it's just not working for them. Many of them may attend church with a happy smile pasted on their face, but there isn't any real joy inside. They attend out of a posture of duty rather than delight, and what they feel inside church doors is loneliness and isolation. They are afraid to voice their questions, because the high-closure culture around them has made them feel like asking questions isn't something "good Christians" do.

The danger to this insight is that we could seek to become more creative or fun in an effort to engage in a spiritual transaction with nonbelievers much like the seeker movement did in the nineties. We don't want our actions to become simple window dressing instead of an actual way of engaging with our communities. Trying to bait-and-switch the Spiritually Curious with faux creativity may very well leave them even more skeptical of Christianity's claims. We cannot pursue creativity as a calculated tactic or strategy to draw in non-Christians. Rather, we should seek the kingdom, endeavoring to create heaven on earth, because that is what we are called to do.

9

Faithful Presence
in Our Communities

The nation of Israel was in turmoil, and the country was divided into two factions: those who supported David and those who supported his rival, King Saul's son, Ish-Bosheth. In 1 Chronicles 12, as David's army marches toward Jerusalem to claim the throne and unite Israel under David's rule, we see warriors from various tribes and factions begin to gather around David's cause.

The men of Issachar stand out among this group; they are praised for their wisdom and ability to "[understand] the times" (v. 32). They knew what Israel ought to do and how to lead the people of Israel to do it. They had a clear understanding of God's will and were able to discern the future course of events. Because of their unique gifts, David made sure to include them in his leadership team, knowing their insight would be priceless in times of war.

The characterization of the men of Issachar is not very detailed in the Bible. However, we can infer much from their tribe's general history. Issachar was one of the twelve tribes of Israel, and the tribe was known for producing industrious and diligent people. They were also known for their agricultural practices, which could explain why they were able to perceive the times and seasons so accurately. They were a tribe of men who understood their environment and knew how best to utilize their resources to work efficiently. It's safe to assume these were the kind of guys who implicitly inspire trust. We've probably all met men and women who just seem to exude competence—the kind of people everyone else just naturally gravitates toward. The men of Issachar were this kind of people.

Although brief, the men of Issachar's mention in the Bible holds great significance for us today—especially for those in roles as church leaders. Our country, our world, is going through rapid changes. The challenges we are facing today require the wisdom and insight of the men of Issachar—knowing what to do and how to lead people effectively.

In fact, for this reason, this passage and the people of Issachar are often referenced by my friends at Barna as a scriptural example for their work. As David Kinnaman puts it, "Social research as we know it today is more sophisticated, but its purpose is often the same: to understand the times and know what to do. This isn't just a biblical precedent, but a pressing need for the Church at large—and for your church too—in an era in which people are drifting away from and questioning the relevance of faith. Data should matter to faith leaders because people matter. Through this lens, percentages become glimpses into the backgrounds, beliefs, challenges and hopes of individuals. They become tools to better understand the world around us and how your people, your church and you as their leader exist within it."[1]

For a couple centuries now, Christians in the United States have enjoyed a dominant role in shaping much of our culture. The rapid pace of change, however, is exposing the fragile faith of many who identify as Christians. Many Christians are finding themselves unsure of what to think or believe in this quickly evolving culture. Many have been hurt or have confused a faith in Jesus Christ with certain political or social movements in ways that have kept them from fully exploring their faith. And as we've seen, many have inadvertently built their faith on a house of cards, liable to crumble at the first sign of trouble. Our job now as leaders in the church is to help reframe discipleship so that Christians might build resilience, not only for themselves, but so they might engage and influence a broken world that needs the good news of the gospel as much as ever.

In this chapter, I hope to do the work of a modern-day son of Issachar by recovering a biblical framework for how we as Christians see ourselves as disciples in this changing world. This framework recognizes our minority position in the culture while also being mindful of our majority position in many places of power, and it encourages us to still care deeply about opening the door of faith to those who are curious about it.

Digital Babylon, Exiles, and the Practice of Faithful Presence

In *Faith for Exiles*, David Kinnaman and I unpacked the identity shift the church in America has experienced. While the identity phenomenon brought on by globalization, the internet, and immigration has impacted nations across the globe, the unique origin story of the church in the United States—which is rooted in the Puritans' escape from the Church of England—has repercussions for the American church today. We've been shaped by a sense of calling that has, in its excesses, veered into self-importance. The "city on a hill" mythos of Matthew 5:14 is so pervasive and woven into white Protestantism, which has been the dominant worldview in the U.S., that it can be hard for us to even recognize it. We are often like a fish unaware of the water we swim in until we encounter another culture, subculture, or worldview that throws this into question.

Many of my dearest friends are missionary kids, or "MKs." Generally, these kids were raised in a different culture than the one they were born into but never became full citizens of their new homelands. They grew up not particularly belonging to any country or culture. This phenomenon is known as being a *third culture kid.* You have your country of birth that your family's culture came from and that you are often anchored to, the culture in which your family lives, and then perhaps even another culture where you attend boarding school. I've learned so much from my friends with these backgrounds. While they often share the pain of not knowing where they belong, they also offer great insight into my own assumptions. We all have certain cultural filters for interpreting the world around us, but third culture kids are often excessively aware of these cultural filters and well-equipped to challenge them. These and other intercultural relationships I enjoy have helped me in so many ways to gain a bigger picture of God and what he is doing in the world.

The reality is that few Americans travel cross-culturally, and if they do, it is rarely with any depth. It takes more than a long weekend in Tokyo to truly grasp what makes Japan a special place to the people who live there. It takes more than a sightseeing trip to the Great Pyramid to understand the lives of the Egyptian people. It takes weeks and months abroad to truly experience what is known as "culture shock." This is the phenomenon that occurs when we are deprived of our cultural norms for an extended period of time. The longer we stay in a different country, the more we become aware of the way of life, culture, and attitudes that shaped us back home, and the more we become aware that those things are not necessarily universal realities for all humanity. It can be a profoundly disorienting sensation. But in my experience, it's almost always a healthy one.

This has become an even more complex phenomenon in the digital world. Whatever sense of place we find when we engage the world through our screens is easily disrupted. Our own cultural boundaries are far more porous online. In this online world of digital Babylon, we can experience culture shock from the relative comfort of our own homes. We are no longer in the mythos of America as the "city on a hill." We are connected to diverse subcultures within our own country—not to mention the rest of the world. And the traditional power structures that kept the mythos alive no longer control the narrative. This culture shock has led to some unhealthy coping mechanisms, with some well-meaning Christians striving to retain a sense of control. It has also led to the church becoming disoriented. While the discomfort is real and there may be a desire to return life to "normal," to make it all "great" again like it used to be, we need to realize that what is happening is a reality check. It's a wake-up call to see life as it is, connect with what God is doing in the here and now, and discover how we can join him in the work.

As we unpacked digital Babylon in *Faith for Exiles*, we stressed the importance of recovering the theology of the exile. If we as a church have lost anything over the last decade, it is our understanding of this particular theology. It's not too late to find it again.

Learning to Live as Exiles

In the Bible, the covenantal relationship between God and Israel set them up as a unique nation, and Jerusalem became the archetype of an incarnational city—where the presence of God and people dwelled together. The disobedience of Judah, the southern kingdom of Israel, allowed for Babylon, another archetypal city, to overpower and enslave it. This led to Judah, with its covenantal culture, to have to live under the authority of a nation that did not acknowledge God and was in fact outside the covenant. Here we see the challenges Judah and some specific citizens faced as they navigated their devotion to God in a godless culture—a culture that sometimes put that devotion to the test.

Throughout the Old Testament and into the New, Scripture shows examples of the Jewish people living in exile

OLD TESTAMENT EXILE	NEW TESTAMENT EXILE
Raised "at home"	Never been home
Exileship result of disobedience / captivity / trauma	Exileship a result of salvation
Israel as nation among nations	Heaven is not of this earth; its citizens are distributed across many nations
Israel a hope for nations	Christians a hope for the world
Babylon	The world = Any human institution that shifts our loyalty from God to its idolatrous systems, values, and beliefs
	Jesus as exile, to show us the way home
Awaiting the Messiah	Awaiting the return of Christ and the establishment of the kingdom
Putting lives on the line for moments of epic trust	Putting lives on the line in moments of epic trust
Loyalty to God, subversive only when loyalty is questioned	Loyalty to God, subversive only when loyalty is questioned
Seeking the good of Babylon through prayer and deed	Seeking the welfare of the world through demonstration of good and the hope of the gospel

Source: Mark Matlock

under the rule of different nations. After Pentecost, as Christianity begins to spread, we see a new framework given to the Christian, who is without an earthly nation and living in a constant state of exile until the return of Christ and the creation of a new heaven and a new earth.

When David and I introduced the idea of digital Babylon in *Faith for Exiles*, some readers I interacted with struggled with the Old Testament concept of the exile in light of the New Testament. In the preceding chart, I've made a comparison of exileship in the Old Testament to that in the New Testament that hopefully you will find helpful. While some circumstances differ, they are very much consistent with one another.

Our New Citizenship

"But our citizenship is in heaven," Paul wrote to the congregation in Philippi (Phil. 3:20). When we trust in Christ, we no longer belong to this world; our citizenship changes. Not only are we regenerated in the Spirit, or born again, we are also now "naturalized"—not to the kingdoms of the earth but to the kingdom of heaven. This is a remarkable reality and theme of the New Testament, and it is one that we do not live into enough.

Our Status Is Resident Alien

First Peter 2:11–12 states, "Dear friends, I urge you, as foreigners and exiles, to abstain from sinful desires, which wage war against your soul. Live such good lives among the pagans that, though they accuse you of doing wrong, they may see your good deeds and glorify God on the day he visits us."

Since we no longer belong to this world and are naturalized citizens of heaven, our status changes. Christians are a nationless people on earth: we don't belong anywhere. We may live on earth (at least for now), but we belong to Christ Jesus and his kingdom. This status change is so strong that it should shape how we live in the neighborhoods and cities around us. Peter tells the early church that, ideally, people—even the people who accuse them of doing wrong—end up glorifying God because of all the good they see Christians do.

We Have New Authority and a New Role

"We are therefore Christ's ambassadors, as though God were making his appeal through us," says 2 Corinthians 5:20.

I've had the privilege to meet several foreign ambassadors. They represent their nation—its sovereignty, culture, and people—in foreign lands. They act on the interests of their nation and display the customs of their country. While they respect the laws of the country they reside in—maybe live in for decades—they do not assimilate into it. They are there to represent their government's interest. They are ultimately under the authority of their native country, no matter how far away they actually live from it.

This is a helpful way for us to think about our status as Christians. Every person who experiences the saving grace of God through Jesus Christ is now living in exile in this world. This idea held significant meaning to New Testament Christians. It impacted how they lived and the influence they had on their local communities and the world's nations.

Understanding Exile in a Democracy

Recognizing our exile status as Christians becomes a little more complicated in a country like the United States. The wonderful experiment called *democracy* and the immigrant origins of the United States have unintentionally blurred the lines for many American Christians in understanding what biblical exileship should look like. The immigration to North America by the Puritans who were escaping perceived religious persecution created a new narrative of the "city on a hill." Some of them started to think of this new country as the New Jerusalem.

Most of these Christians did not come to America with missionary pursuits—to be ambassadors of the faith and share the Good News with the people who already lived here. Rather, they wanted to establish a new colony.

As what ultimately became the American Revolution approached, there were theological disagreements around how to apply the biblical teaching about authority to the growing frustrations with England under King George. There were deep theological disagreements about the application of Romans 13 to revolutionary thought. While most Americans seemed to share widespread dissatisfaction with British rule, many argued for taking a less violent, more patient approach to change and were concerned about the way the Bible was being used to justify revolutionary thinking. Revolutionary-minded Americans insulted these Christians as "loyalist preachers," and most of their writings were destroyed by the Patriots in a swell of national fervor. It has been only in recent decades that their sermons have begun to circulate.

Today, it is common for Americans to make toothless vows to "leave the country" if a presidential election doesn't go the way they like. But when the Revolution prevailed, many of these early Americans really did leave in droves. Some 60,000 to 80,000 left the colonies after the American Revolution, many of them well-educated and wealthy.[2] This represented 15–20 percent of the U.S. population, no small number, rapidly changing the nascent social fabric of the country. For the remaining American Christians, a new era of Christianity would evolve under democratic rule.

In some ways, it's easier to see exileship under authoritarian rule. But under a democratic republic where authority at least theoretically rests with the people rather than the divine right of the monarchy or brute military force, recognizing your exileship becomes more challenging.

For example, it is popular and accepted to embrace a theological perspective of "dual citizenship" in the U.S., whether or not we are aware we hold this view. It's widely believed that America has been a nation under God, founded on Christian principles, and it is therefore healthy to love God and country with equal fervor. For Christians who take this view, it is sometimes difficult to tell where being a good patriot ends and being an obedient follower of Jesus begins. In this way, we are seduced out of living in exile.

But if we take the more biblical view, understanding that we are in exile while living in this world, then we cannot be "dual citizens" of the United States or any other country. We can have only one allegiance, and that is to King Jesus and his kingdom. Perhaps this confusion over dual citizenship helps us better understand the culture war many American Christians are engaged in. We are stuck in a cycle of seeking political influence rather than living the assignment given to us as ambassadors. We are trying to force our country to become something it can never be.

A Theology of Faithful Presence

I have lived my entire life in states on the southern U.S. border or the western coast. As a fourth-generation American, I am quite aware of my immigrant past and the incredible opportunity and spiritual heritage the U.S. gave to my father's family. When my great-grandmother journeyed to the U.S. as an elementary schooler, her family was poor. They didn't have much wealth, education, position of power, or influence; all they had was their presence. As it turned out, their presence was enough.

I've seen immigrants come into the U.S. the same way, and without political or economic power they change the landscape of the culture. How? Simply by their presence. Their influence is not money or position. It's simply their physical being. It's their proximity to the people around them.

Indeed, this is the way Christians are called to do such good deeds: as aliens and strangers. Since we, too, are strangers in this world, maybe we can learn from this powerful—if subtle—way of influencing the world. Perhaps a missed way of shaping culture is that of faithful presence. In 2010, James Davison Hunter popularized this term in *To Change the World*. In an interview with *Christianity Today* about the book, Hunter says, "Faithful presence isn't new; it's just something we need to recover."[3] The following Four Tenets of Faithful Presence are my attempt to craft such a practical theology for myself, and I hope it may be helpful to you as well.

Four Tenets of Faithful Presence

1. As Christians we live in this world as exiles, loyal citizens of heaven and its King, Jesus. We belong to no earthly nation and reside as aliens and strangers in the world: we are ambassadors of heaven.

2. Our greatest power comes from the authority granted us by Jesus and is seen in his example of a faithful presence: he lived on earth as it is in heaven. We will never perfectly emulate his example but can do our best to shine forth.

3. We seek the welfare of the nation where we reside, specifically paying attention to the marginalized, smaller communities and residents.

4. We take advantage of every opportunity to participate in our place of residence, respectful of its local authority as long as that does not demand disloyalty to our King and his kingdom, our true home.

When I've shared this with other Christian leaders, they often attack this approach as being "passive." I understand their criticism. Christian leaders rightfully want to be part of a godly movement, and the word *presence* doesn't exactly scream "change the world." However, "faithful presence" is anything but passive.

Developing Our Faithful Presence in the Public Square

As a facilitator, I get the chance to hear from a variety of groups across the country. A favorite warm-up question I have asked over the last decade is, "What in the last couple years has surprised you most in your ministry?"

The most common response of this decade had something to do with the speed at which same-sex marriages have been accepted by the culture. And indeed, opinion surveys show that the cultural shift on this subject has been dramatic. For decades, most Americans did not approve of the legalization of same-sex marriages. And then, in a very short amount of time, they did. Church denominations began to split over the matter, and mainstream cultural critiques of the LGBTQ+ community instantly became angry, loud, and toxic in ways that they had not been before.

There are few radical shifts in opinion I've seen in my lifetime, and the church—in general—was not at all prepared for all that would be unleashed when the Defense of Marriage Act was overturned by the Supreme Court. Being "antihomosexual" was one of the top behaviors associated with Christians that was identified in *unChristian* by David Kinnaman and Gabe Lyons.[4] Not "loving." Not "compassionate toward those they disagree with." Just "antihomosexual." In this arena (as in many others), Christians have developed a far more notable reputation for what we stand against than what we stand for.

This issue more than any other has required us to search for a richer model to live out our faith. One major reason may be the lack of nuance we bring to our interpretation of Scripture and how we live out that interpretation in the world around us.

I have an ongoing conversation about faith and culture with Darrell Bock, executive director of Cultural Engagement and senior research professor of New Testament Studies at Dallas Theological Seminary. Over breakfast in Dallas, Darrell explained to me that there are three primary "lenses" Christians need to see through to interpret Scripture.

The Theological Lens

This is the lens we look through most often as we seek to understand the nature of God, ourselves, and creation.

The theological lens is our attempt to distill the ultimate truths that create our worldview, and the main question to consider is, **What is the knowledge God gives us through special revelation?**

Remember, this lens provides an interpretation of the truth; it isn't the truth itself. God's revelation is perfect. Our interpretation is not. It's an attempt to do the best that we can do, and we must humbly remind ourselves that we are not infallible. This is why two Christians can be equally sincere in their spiritual convictions and yet still come away with different understandings of what the Bible says.

While almost everything springs from the work of the theological lens, it provides little direct application on its own. Here we may learn that God is holy, that humans are sinful, that humans need salvation. While the other two lenses are indeed "theological" (because everything we do is in some sense a theological practice), they are asking different questions of the text.

The Pastoral Lens

The pastoral lens is what we use to determine how to apply the truth of Scripture to our lives and the lives of others. The main question here is, **How do I help others be reconciled to God and live sanctified lives?** Pastors use this lens to help shepherd their flock—or an individual—toward holy living.

Sometimes the pastoral lens is very clear, other times less so. While the theological lens tells us that God is holy, humans are sinful, and Jesus atoned for our sin, the pastoral lens helps us confess our sin and experience salvation. The pastoral lens helps us deal with temptation. The pastoral lens is focused on our connection to God: how it can be forged, strengthened, and—when necessary—repaired.

It also asks how we can care for people and love them well as we seek to reflect God's care and character as we reflect his image. It is possible to be right in what we believe but handle it wrong pastorally, so that we still are wrong in how we engage. This pastoral care really matters. In fact, in some cases, it matters as much or more than being right. (Recall the tips in chapter 6 about how to engage the Spiritually Curious.)

Many of Paul's epistles are spent dealing with how to help the church live as Christians. His letters were giving divine guidance on how the church should become more like Jesus. While such passages are brimming with truth, Paul's day was different than our day. In our modern times, a situation will often present itself for which there is not a clear passage to guide us.

The Public Square Lens

A third, less-used lens is needed to know how we apply Scripture to the cultural context we live in. This is especially relevant to our discussion of the Spiritually Curious. Here the pertinent question is, **How should we as Christians live in a world that doesn't believe as we do?**

In a nation that protects free speech and the exercise of religion, it isn't possible, or appropriate, to impose values that are implicitly validated by biblical insights alone. This doesn't mean that these insights and values must be muzzled though. Consider Daniel's plea in Daniel 1, which we unpacked in the last chapter. He and his friends do not impose their Jewish laws on others, even though they choose not to participate in the Babylonian rituals themselves. The freedom to practice, or not to, is what is important to them. In the case of the food from the king's table, Daniel appeals to a test to show that the Jewish dietary restrictions are actually beneficial beyond their religious significance.

Where possible, we should view issues similarly, through the lens of the public sphere. We should fight for the freedom to practice religious values or not and also, where and when possible, appeal to the general benefit of God's wisdom on a given matter. In this way, we showcase God's common grace, and we honor him.

All Three Lenses

In Paul's letter to the church at Corinth, we see these three lenses at work in what can sometimes be a confusing passage. In it, we see Paul addressing a sexual immorality issue that has not only been allowed to continue but has been allowed to continue by Christians who think doing so is the "gracious" thing to do:

> It is actually reported that there is sexual immorality among you, and of a kind that even pagans do not tolerate: A man is sleeping with his father's wife. And you are proud! Shouldn't you rather have gone into mourning and have put out of your fellowship the man who has been doing this? (1 Cor. 5:1–2)

This strange passage may seem to have very little to do with our modern churches. But if we look closely, we can see Paul employ all three "lenses" in unison, and we can learn to do the same in our own lives and ministry.

Note that Paul mentions the egregious nature of the sin—that even those who are pagan wouldn't accept this act of incest. Paul is acknowledging two realities: both life within the church (the pastoral lens) and life outside, among the "pre-believers" or "nonbelievers." It is this life outside the church which (primarily) requires the public square lens.

Paul continues: "So when you are assembled and I am with you in spirit, and the power of our Lord Jesus is present, hand this man over to Satan for the destruction of the flesh, so that his spirit may be saved on the day of the Lord" (vv. 4–5). In other words, Paul's desired end result in all of this is that the man would be reconciled to God. Here we see a pastoral lens application based on insight from reading Scripture through the theological lens. It's because Paul understands the situation theologically that he is able to also understand it pastorally.

Then he returns to the public square and looks at the situation through a different lens: "I wrote to you in my letter not to associate with sexually immoral people—not at all meaning the people of this world who are immoral, or the greedy and swindlers, or idolaters. In that case you would have to leave this world" (vv. 9–10).

This is profound. While Paul is judging the church through his pastoral lens, he's acknowledging there's also a counter-application that will likely seem inconsistent with all he is saying.

He goes on:

> But now I am writing to you that you must not associate with anyone who claims to be a brother or sister but is sexually immoral or greedy, an idolater or slanderer, a drunkard or swindler. Do not even eat with such people.

What business is it of mine to judge those outside the church? Are you not to judge those inside? God will judge those outside. "Expel the wicked person from among you." (vv. 11–13)

This brief example of Paul's instruction has been misused in the church to deliver alarmingly harsh church discipline devoid of any grace and mercy. New Testament teaching on church discipline was intended for small, close-knit congregations, and many of our attempts to apply it to our megachurch culture have been fraught with disaster.

But church discipline is not my focus here. I want to point out that Paul's rebuke was not directed at the sinful member of the body, but the leaders of the church and the broader body. The body of believers was making a mockery of God's grace. The offender did not have a repentant heart. Paul's objective was to reconcile the offender and the congregation to God through repentance.

My reason for bringing this up is to point out that there are two standards of accountability here: one for those inside the church and one for those outside it. Our goal for those outside the church is to bring the Good News, the gospel, to others. We want them to first be able to trust in God. There is no future that doesn't begin there.

Finding Common Ground with the Curious

Remember Peter's teaching about living good lives amidst those that do not yet believe? In it, we saw a framework for the lens of the public square: "Live such good lives among the pagans that, though they accuse you of doing wrong, they may see your good deeds and glorify God on the day he visits us" (1 Pet. 2:12).

In my ministry with city gospel movements, I've had to think long and hard about how the church shows up in the city. I've been guided by friends such as Kevin Palau, who has labored for some time in Portland, Oregon, working as a liaison between the faith community and city leadership. For a time, he worked closely with Sam Adams, the first openly gay mayor of a major U.S. city. Once Adams was elected, Kevin and their city movement wanted to meet with him to see how the church could serve the city.

Both Kevin and Mayor Adams will admit there are many things they disagree about. Nevertheless, a friendship developed between the two by focusing on places the city and the church could find common ground.

Finding common ground with people who disagree with us is a fine art that takes some time and practice. But like any art, it's a skill well worth mastering. Here are four questions on which to focus.

1. Where is our common ground?

Tim Muehlhoff, professor of communication at Biola University, wrote in *I Beg to Differ* that society has lost interest in finding common ground and maintaining healthy relationships with people when they disagree on certain things.[5] I couldn't agree more. It's bad enough how quickly we exit the room when we encounter any opinions that are different from ours, but we aren't even entering the room with a desire to find where on the Venn diagram our lives intersect. To engage the Spiritually Curious, we must find those places of intersection.

For Kevin and Mayor Adams, it was the welfare of Portland. They both wanted to see crime decrease, education scores increase, and a greater number of people find affordable housing. While Kevin would also want to see the people of Portland know Jesus, he didn't have to make that a dealbreaker for their partnership. There was plenty in common to stay and build a friendship on.

One of the goals of my research with the curious is to help us see the common ground we share that we can use to build real relationships of trust. The problems facing our country are many, and tackling them effectively requires strategic cooperation. Even if we don't see eye to eye on everything, we still have opportunities to cooperate where we do agree.

2. What might threaten my loyalty to Christ?

It's important to know where the boundaries are. There might be fewer than you think but—as seen in the lives of exiles like Joseph, Daniel, Esther, Shadrach, Meshach, and Abednego—there are boundaries.

We first see Daniel struggling with eating food that goes against Jewish dietary restrictions. But look at how he makes his appeal to Nebuchadnezzar. He appeals on the common ground of good health and offers a test that leads to favor with the king. That was an example of Daniel and his friends navigating a boundary they held.

However, when it came to studying Babylonian literature and customs and even taking Babylonian names that contained the names of false gods, there didn't seem to be an issue. Daniel and his friends didn't pick every single fight. We too can pick our battles wisely and maturely.

Throughout Scripture, we see those who follow God draw their boundary lines around anything that would shift their trust to something other than Christ. We can use that as a helpful guide in drawing our own boundary lines in this culture.

3. What Good News does Jesus bring to the situation?

As bearers of the Good News, we need to ask what changes as a result of finding common ground. As the disciples preached the Good News, Jews who had been overwhelmed by legalistic demands as a means of salvation saw Jesus's death and resurrection as the fulfillment of the promise of a Messiah and the full realization of grace. For the gentiles and the pagans, who knew something in creation had gone wrong and humanity played a part in it, the gospel was freedom from sin and the realization of a relationship with a God that they could know.

When it comes to the public square, does the good of the city require belief in the gospel? While it may be the ultimate goal of our good works, our seeking the social good of others isn't dependent on the gospel alone. We can still find ways to improve people's quality of life—helping to feed the hungry, providing housing for the homeless, and finding resources for those who are financially struggling—before securing their commitment to salvation.

4. What kingdom resources can be used to seek the peace and prosperity of my community?

At the time of the writing of this book, we've just come through the pandemic. New York City was hit harder than most places, losing more lives per capita than any U.S. city.[6]

During this time, the united churches of New York City, across the five boroughs, gave the use of their buildings and networks to distribute goods and services to any person, no strings attached. That's what it means to act through the lens of the public square.

A primary focus of this chapter has been to understand aspects of our discipleship that can strengthen our ability to reach the Spiritually Curious in this age of spiritual openness. Many who are curious have had negative experiences with the church, so enhancing our reputation by living in more Christlike ways in our neighborhoods is critical to our efforts to reach them.

10

Lessons Learned

The subject of curiosity is nothing new. People have always been curious. Ever since God created the forbidden fruit in the garden, humans wanted to know what it would be like to know things like God.

Today, there is an exceptional phenomenon unfolding in the United States—a spiritual curiosity—that demands our attention. It compels us to reassess our approach to church and our role as the church. If we properly understand and graciously engage this phenomenon, the transformation that comes over our churches could be vast.

As we conclude this book, I would like to highlight six key insights that have profoundly impacted my personal journey in understanding spiritual curiosity. I started working on the idea for this book a few years before the pandemic. As the pandemic unfolded, I found myself spending less time at church and more time with people in my neighborhood.

I didn't normally have contact with my neighbors in a spiritual context, and doing so has changed my life. This period of time only confirmed many of the ideas that I had about the Spiritually Curious.

1. God is at work in places where I don't think to look.

A lot of times, I believe that God is working in only specific areas—where there's mission activity or the church is doing a project. But God is also working in the most pagan of places and in the hearts and minds of people who have never thought much about him. So I'm learning to step into every environment with humility, not thinking that I'm bringing something new, but beginning from a posture of trying to figure out what God is already up to in this space. How is God already working in a person's life, or how has he been preparing them for this moment? How can I join an *ongoing process* instead of trying to be the main character in my own project?

This happened with one of my daughter's boyfriends. Keep in mind, this was the first time I'd met this young man, and the question he asked me was, "Mr. Matlock, how do I know when God is pursuing me?" A really bold question for a first-time meeting, but, knowing that I'm a pastor, I think he assumed I was a safe person to talk to about this type of thing.

"So, John, do you feel like God has been pursuing you?" I said.

He related a few encounters he'd had where he felt that a number of things in combination with dating my daughter might mean that God was trying to send a message to him.

I had walked into that encounter just thinking, *Here's a guy who hasn't really grown up in church and has a very mixed background in his faith.* I never thought to ask myself if God was already there or what kind of questions I could ask to discover how God might already be at work in this man's life. How much richer might our interactions be if we could trust that wherever we go and whoever we meet, God both got there ahead of us and will continue to be there long after we're gone.

2. I don't have to be afraid when I'm on unfamiliar turf.

Growing up, I was always told to avoid places where a lot of sinners gathered. So I never went to parties in high school; I tried to hang around only the most Christian of friends. Maybe, when I was younger, that was a good path to be on. And there's no question that being around places where there isn't a strong spiritual presence can be uncomfortable for a Christian. However, we don't need to be afraid to be in those places.

In fact, I need to be asking myself, Why am I not in those places more often? I used to point out the fact that I didn't drink, thinking that was a sign of holiness and purity. As I approached my forties, I started sipping alcohol a little here and there. At that stage in my life, I felt like I had a pretty good head on my shoulders, but I was amazed to see how not being afraid of alcohol or signaling that I was against alcohol opened opportunities for me to be invited into circles where people who needed Jesus were hanging out, getting to know each other, and forming deep bonds.

I got involved in conversations I never would have been involved in before.

I am not saying that we shouldn't be careful about things we know might be a temptation for us. For example, a person who has struggled with addiction has every reason to avoid situations where alcohol will be present. But in my case, I realized that something I thought was a sign of my holiness was actually preventing me from being in the places where Jesus wanted me to be. We've got to be less insular if we want to reach people. Getting off your own turf is a great first step.

3. Trusting God is more important than doing things for God.

I've known this all my life, and it's been shared with me in many different teachings on grace. But I think it's only been through trying to put myself in places with people who are lost, who don't know the Lord, who aren't defiant of him but just don't know him, that I'm realizing that trusting in him is so much more important than doing things for him.

This isn't just about my relationship with God; it's also what I project and place on other people as well. You see, when I think that doing things for God is more important than trusting him, I lead others to focus on their behavior more than I lead them to focus on their relationship with Jesus. No matter what I say I believe, I communicate that Christianity is nothing more than a series of dos and don'ts. In fact, what is most important to me is that they trust in Jesus. I truly believe that when they trust in Jesus, enter into a relationship with him, and truly experience his grace, they are going to experience God in a life-changing way. My finger wagging and checklists aren't really going to have an impact on their life, or may have a negative impact, so I have to keep a correct focus. The most important thing is trusting in God.

I once heard an African word for "trust" that meant leaning on a tree and not falling. I've never been able to find a source for this, but I love that image of being able to take all of your weight and lean it completely on something, knowing it's going to hold you. That's how I try to think about my relationship with God and what I'm trying to help people who don't know Jesus to find. I want them to put the full weight of their life and trust in God, letting him take them where he needs them to go. I'm just there to shepherd them along the way and to help them understand what the Scripture says. If someone is in a real, trusting relationship with the living God, the behavior part takes care of itself.

4. It's better to know Jesus than know about him.

In many ways, this is related to number three, which delved into how trusting God is more important than doing things for him. But knowing Jesus *is* better than just knowing about him. I know that sounds really obvious to those of us who have been Christians for some time. However, I've found that there are far more Christians who *know about* Jesus than actually *know* him. There are people who don't know Jesus themselves but are teaching our pastors how to do ministry. These people may know a lot *about* Jesus (head knowledge), but they don't know him (heart knowledge). We have to keep in mind that the most important thing is that people trust and know Jesus. Not as some distant, unknowable magic man in the clouds but as someone with whom they are in a real relationship. Someone with whom they are experiencing life each and every day.

5. There are fewer people hostile to Christianity than I thought.

Yes, there are people who are very hostile toward Christianity. You may have unpleasant stories of meeting those people. However, there are not nearly as many as I used to think. I tend to find that even those who are actively hostile toward Christianity are more than willing to spend time with me. This has given me great boldness in my relationships and encounters with others.

There's a pastor in Singapore whose approach to strangers, when he meets them, whether on a plane or in a cab or anywhere else, is to say, "Wow, you must be the luckiest person in the world."

They say, "Why would you say that?"

And then he says, "Well, there are six billion people on the planet, and today, God put you next to a Christian pastor."

I haven't tried out that line yet, but I do think it's a brilliant way to think about life. God has placed us in the paths of all those we encounter, and they likely aren't as hostile to his message as we might assume. But we must think differently about how we're delivering his message. It's not about closing the deal; it's realizing the role that you might get to play in their journey on the path of spiritual discovery. It's about recognizing that we don't need to be ashamed of our faith. We need to realize that our faith should literally affect every part of our life: how we live and our interactions with every person we meet.

6. Engaging the Spiritually Curious takes time.

And it takes relational work. The current science on relationships says that our cognitive capacity can maintain only 150 friends—and only five are close ones.[1] People have scoffed at this. They've said that's ridiculous. But over and over again, science has proven this to be true—we can really manage only a certain number of close relationships.

I have five thousand Facebook friends. I can go through that list of five thousand and probably tell you how I know about three-fifths of them. I could probably even tell you how I met most of them. A big reason I have five thousand Facebook friends is because my profile became active when Facebook was just starting, and during that time I was traveling the country speaking at conferences and camps and meeting lots of young people year after year. I've never been the type to hide backstage; I always interact with the crowds before and after speaking engagements. So I know a lot of people.

But I can confirm that while I can connect names and faces and tell stories about thousands of people, I don't have the kind of relationship with them that I have with my closest friends.

The reason I bring this up is because we can't view evangelism as transactional. If God designed our hardware to manage a certain capacity of relationships, he must know there are limits to the number of people we can evangelize as well.

A huge issue with many of our modern evangelism methods that don't give the time to reach the Spiritually Curious is our failure to recognize that capacity is the problem. We need more people sharing their faith with the people closest to them instead of trying to find ways for people to share their faith with hundreds of people they barely know. If every Christian was actively living out their faith (heaven on earth, a faithful presence), more people would be reached.

Which means we're all going to need to be involved in this work. If we are leaders of churches, ministries, or outreach efforts—or we have staff who are going out and sharing their faith—we need to make sure we're doing things where everybody's involved. We need follow-up opportunities for long-term connection. I don't believe that the shotgun approach of bringing in large groups and trying to share Christ through a large group activity is really effective anymore, and it's certainly not the way to reach the Spiritually Curious. Nor do I believe that sending throngs of young people out to do evangelism in the city streets for a week produces long-term outcomes. We need people who are living fully present in their cities to do this work. This work cannot be the exclusive domain of pastors and other church leaders. Rather, we need people in all walks of life to join in this vital effort. We need people who are sharing their faith with those they actually know and can come alongside for times of deeper exploration.

We, as a church, need to teach and embrace a whole new way of disciple-making, recognizing that people have only so many relationships that they can manage at every level. We want to make sure that we aren't so insularly focused that we don't give the Spiritually Curious the time, respect, and attention they deserve to be guided toward finding and following Jesus.

I hope this book has been an encouragement to you about the hopefulness of the landscape in which we are ministering and that your mind is thinking about ways to engage those who are curious, even if it means reimagining how you are currently doing outreach. I hope that someday when we are in the kingdom of heaven together, on this renewed and restored earth, many people with us will be able to connect their coming to faith to a shift in thinking that helped us better engage their spiritual curiosity.

Asking Good Questions

Journey with Barna Group through some of the recent milestones and turning points in our ongoing study of faith and curiosity in the U.S.

Meeting the Spiritually Open Moment

Though metrics like Christian affiliation and church attendance in the U.S. have been on a downward slide, Barna studies in recent years still give Christian leaders cause for hope. Particularly since 2020, we have observed what might be thought of as a strengthening "spiritually open moment" (in fact, 44 percent told us in late 2022 that they were more open to God than they were before the pandemic).

% of U.S. adults who...

⊸ All adults ⊸■ Gen Z → Millennials ⊣ Gen X ⊸o Boomers

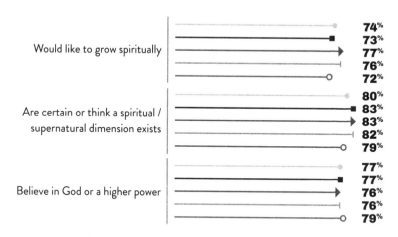

Would like to grow spiritually
- 74%
- 73%
- 77%
- 76%
- 72%

Are certain or think a spiritual / supernatural dimension exists
- 80%
- 83%
- 83%
- 82%
- 79%

Believe in God or a higher power
- 77%
- 77%
- 76%
- 76%
- 79%

n=2,000 U.S. adults, October 21–31, 2022. Source: Barna Group

Notice how this spiritual hunger seems consistent across all generations. This tracks with other Barna research among teens and young adults, both around the world and in the U.S. At present, openness is such a defining trait of today's teenagers that we've begun to refer to them as "the open generation."

The Open Generation

We see that teens are generally open to Jesus, the Bible, and justice. Further, their commitments to these three things are interwoven and increase together.

The majority of Gen Z in the U.S., both teens and young adults, say they are motivated to continue learning about Jesus throughout the rest of their life. Even Gen Z non-Christians exhibit this openness: nearly half are at least somewhat motivated to continue learning about Jesus throughout their lives.

Throughout the rest of your life, how motivated are you to continue learning more about Jesus Christ?

● Very motivated ● Somewhat motivated

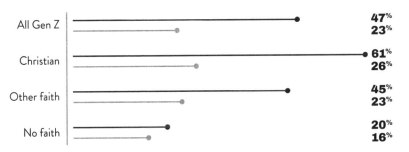

	Very motivated	Somewhat motivated
All Gen Z	47%	23%
Christian	61%	26%
Other faith	45%	23%
No faith	20%	16%

n=2,025 U.S. Gen Z teens and adults, July 21–August 24, 2021. Source: Barna Group

Knowledge and reverence do not always translate to commitment—but it's encouraging that teens and young adults think warmly of Jesus, are curious about his character, and believe he represents love, hope, care, generosity, and trustworthiness.

What People Are Searching For

So, what are the desired paths and destinations for people on their spiritual journeys? Mainly, hope and peace. The church has an opportunity to address these deeply felt needs of the soul in turbulent times.

When you consider your spiritual beliefs, what would you say you are looking for?

◯ Denotes a top three response

● All U.S. adults ● Christian ● Other faith ● No faith

	All U.S. adults	Christian	Other faith	No faith
Inner peace	37%	40%	35%	30%
Hope	35%	40%	31%	24%
Healing	30%	32%	31%	22%
Forgiveness	30%	37%	27%	12%
Truth	29%	31%	33%	23%
Purpose	29%	32%	26%	22%
Guidance	28%	32%	27%	15%
Growth	26%	26%	28%	23%
Meaning	25%	28%	23%	20%
Salvation	25%	32%	18%	6%

n=2,005 U.S. adults, December 13–22, 2022. Source: Barna Group

Looking for Answers

Openness may lead to curiosity and connection—it also leaves room for questions and doubt. For instance, people of any faith identity might encounter hypocrisy, suffering, and conflict as obstacles in their beliefs.

Do any of the following cause you to doubt Christian beliefs? Select all that apply.

All U.S. adults	Christian	Other faith	No faith
34% The hypocrisy of religious people	**31%** Human suffering	**35%** The hypocrisy of religious people	**53%** The hypocrisy of religious people
33% Human suffering	**28%** Conflict in the world	**30%** Human suffering	**43%** One religion can't have all the answers
30% Conflict in the world	**28%** The hypocrisy of religious people	**29%** Conflict in the world	**42%** The negative reputation of religious institutions

n=1,501 U.S. adults, February 19–23, 2023. Source: Barna Group

But doubt doesn't have to be a deal-breaker. In fact, doubt is often seen as a necessary part of life's journey, or even a good thing to tackle. People tell Barna they highly value honesty and openness in their belief systems—and in faith leaders.

It is common for some people to experience doubts around their spiritual or religious beliefs. Which of the following comes closest to how you feel about these kinds of doubts?

● All U.S. adults ● Christian ● Other faith ● No faith

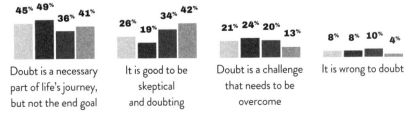

Doubt is a necessary part of life's journey, but not the end goal	It is good to be skeptical and doubting	Doubt is a challenge that needs to be overcome	It is wrong to doubt
45% 49% 36% 41%	26% 19% 34% 42%	21% 24% 20% 13%	8% 8% 10% 4%

n=2,005 U.S. adults, December 13–22, 2022. Source: Barna Group

Continued Curiosity:
Other Research & Resources

The Open Generation:
A Global Teens Study

With a trusted group of partners
including Biblica, World Vision,
and Alpha, Barna embarked on the
largest study in its history to better
understand teens in 26 nations. If
you work with young people, explore
the data and a series of global and
country-specific reports at
barna.com/the-open-generation.

The *Spiritually Open* Project

Barna continues to share research, expert interviews, and practical
tools for "cultivating curiosity and conversation about Jesus." Church
leaders, learn more at barna.gloo.us/evangelism with a Barna Access
subscription.

Research and Methodology

Faith for the Curious

This was a survey of 1,501 U.S. adults, conducted online from February 19–23, 2023, via a consumer research panel. The margin of error for the sample is +/−2.3 percent at the 95 percent confidence level. Quotas were set to representation by region, race/ethnicity, education, age, and gender based on census data. Minimal statistical weighting has been applied to maximize sample representation.

External scales that were used in this survey:

- Need for Closure Scale: Webster, D. M., and A. W. Kruglanski. "Individual Differences in Need for Cognitive Closure." *Journal of Personality and Social Psychology* 67, no. 6 (1994): 1049–62.
- Need for Closure Scale: Roets, A., and A. Van Hiel. "Separating Ability from Need: Clarifying the Dimensional Structure of the Need for Closure

Scale." *Personality and Social Psychology Bulletin* 33, no. 2 (2007): 266–80.

- Curiosity Scale: Kashdan T. B., M. W. Gallagher, P. J. Silvia, B. P. Winterstein, W. E. Breen, D. Terhar, M. F. Steger. "The Curiosity and Exploration Inventory-II: Development, Factor Structure, and Psychometrics." *Journal of Research in Personality* 43, no. 6 (2009): 987–98. https://www.sciencedirect.com/science/article/abs/pii/S0092656609001275.

Spiritually Open

This was a survey of 2,005 U.S. adults and teenagers (aged thirteen to seventeen), conducted online from December 13–22, 2022, via a consumer research panel. The margin of error for the sample is +/−2.0 percent at the 95 percent confidence level. Quotas were set to representation by region, race/ethnicity, education, age, and gender based on census data. Minimal statistical weighting has been applied to maximize sample representation.

Acknowledgments

There are so many people who have made this book possible, and without them I couldn't have pulled it together.

First, my lovely wife, Jade, who is always picking up after me so my energy stays focused.

David Kinnaman, one of my closest and trusted friends over the last couple decades—thanks for pushing me to work this project out.

The board of MOVEMENT.ORG—Bob Doll, Rick Lyons, Bishop Claude Alexander, Dan Wolgemuth, Brian Jacks, Jessica Chin, Jim Runyan, Gant Elmore, Josh Balmer, and Ram Gidoomal. I was finishing this book during an interim CEO-ship, and their generous governance allowed me to take the time to complete the book while serving them.

Daniel Copeland, who leads research at Barna and who gave me way more of his Fridays than was warranted to slice and dice the data to get to the bottom of what we were seeing in the culture. Ashley Ekmay who jumped in at the end to help with generating tables and verifying my assumptions. Thank you both!

Alyce Youngblood, executive editor at Barna, who has always encouraged me to "put more Mark" in the book. Tyler Huckabee, for adding some last-minute touches.

The team at Baker that has worked tirelessly to make this book better than the original manuscript warranted—Mark Rice, Rebekah Von Lintel, Eileen Hanson, Robin Turici, and my developmental editor, Jamie Chavez.

Marian Liautaud, who worked tirelessly to help me frame the project and put the initial pitch together—you were the first champion of *Faith for the Curious* and your spirit kept me writing until the very end.

Heidi Rosenblatt, my admin and project manager—Jade and I are so thankful that you are part of our lives, helping steward my ideas into action. You are a trusted partner and friend in this kingdom work. Thank you!

Notes

Chapter 1 A New Way

1. David Kinnaman and Mark Matlock, *Faith for Exiles: 5 Ways for a New Generation to Follow Jesus in Digital Babylon* (Grand Rapids: Baker Books, 2019), 33.

Chapter 2 The Spiritually Curious

1. "Signs of Decline & Hope among Key Metrics of Faith," Barna Group, March 4, 2020, https://www.barna.com/research/changing-state-of-the-church/.

2. Interview with David John Seel Jr. conducted by Mark Matlock on August 4, 2022.

3. D. E. Berlyne, "A Theory of Human Curiosity," *British Journal of Psychology* 45, no. 3 (August 1954): 180–91.

4. George Loewenstein, "The Psychology of Curiosity: A Review and Reinterpretation," *Psychological Bulletin* 116, no. 1 (1994): 75–98, https://www.cmu.edu/dietrich/sds/docs/loewenstein/PsychofCuriosity.pdf.

5. For more reading on the five dimensions of curiosity, check out the following links: Todd B. Kashdan, David J. Disabato, Fallon R. Goodman, and Carl Naughton, "The Five Dimensions of Curiosity," *Harvard Business Review*, September–October 2018, https://hbr.org/2018/09/the-five-dimensions-of-curiosity; Todd B. Kashdan, "What Are the Five Dimensions of Curiosity?," PsychologyToday.com, January 2, 2018, https://www.psychologytoday.com/us/blog/curious/201801/what-are-the-five-dimensions-curiosity.

6. Kinnaman and Matlock, *Faith for Exiles*, 17.

Chapter 3 The Curious Skeptic

1. William Barclay, *The Gospel of Luke* (Philadelphia: Westminster John Knox Press, 1975), 117–18.
2. C. S. Lewis, "A Christmas Sermon for Pagans," *Strand Magazine*, December 1946, 30–33.
3. Lewis, "Christmas Sermon for Pagans."
4. Lewis, "Christmas Sermon for Pagans."
5. C. S. Lewis in Don Giovanni Calabria, *The Latin Letters of C. S. Lewis* (South Bend, IN: St. Augustine's Press, 2016), 90–93. © Copyright CS Lewis Pte Ltd.

Chapter 4 A Curious Culture

1. Brian Grazer, *A Curious Mind: The Secret to a Bigger Life* (New York: Simon & Schuster, 2016), 98–100.
2. D. M. Webster and A. W. Kruglanski, "Individual Differences in Need for Cognitive Closure," *Journal of Personality and Social Psychology* 67, no. 6 (1994): 1049–62; A. Roets and A. Van Hiel, "Item Selection and Validation of a Brief, 15-Item Version of the Need for Closure Scale," *Personality and Individual Differences* 50, no. 1 (2011): 90–94.
3. "What Do We Do with Doubt?," Barna Group, February 28, 2023, https://barna.gloo.us/articles/spiritually-open-issue-1. (Subscription required.)

Chapter 5 A Curious Posture

1. Todd Kashdan, *Curious? Discover the Missing Ingredient to a Fulfilling Life* (New York: Harper, 2009), 39.
2. Kashdan, *Curious?*, 25.

Chapter 6 Engaging the Spiritually Curious

1. "Soul Searching: What Spirituality Means to Americans Today," Barna Group, March 27, 2023, https://barna.gloo.us/articles/spiritually-open-issue-2/. (Subscription required.)
2. "What to Know about Spiritually Open Non-Christians," Barna Group, June 4, 2023, https://barna.gloo.us/articles/spiritually-open-issue-4. (Subscription required.)
3. "How Churches Can Coach Christians to Share Their Faith," Barna Group, July 30, 2023, https://barna.gloo.us/articles/spiritually-open-issue-6. (Subscription required.)
4. Kinnaman and Matlock, *Faith for Exiles*, 143.

5. "For Good Conversations about Faith, Try Talking Less," Barna Group, July 4, 2023, https://barna.gloo.us/articles/spiritually-open-issue -5. (Subscription required.)

6. Barna Group, *Reviving Evangelism: Current Realities That Demand a New Vision for Sharing Faith* (Ventura, CA: Barna Group, 2019).

Chapter 7 The Search for Something More

1. Linda Rodriguez McRobbie, "The Strange and Mysterious History of the Ouija Board," Smithsonianmag.com, October 27, 2013, https:// www.smithsonianmag.com/history/the-strange-and-mysterious-history -of-the-ouija-board-5860627/.

2. McRobbie, "Strange and Mysterious History of the Ouija Board."

3. Personal communication with A. Bjerke on July 6, 2023.

4. Personal communication with A. Bjerke on July 6, 2023.

Chapter 8 On Earth as It Is in Heaven

1. C. S. Lewis, *The Weight of Glory: And Other Addresses* (New York: HarperOne, 2001), 26. © Copyright CS Lewis Pte Ltd.

2. Interview with David John Seel Jr. conducted by Mark Matlock on August 4, 2022.

3. Randy Alcorn, *Heaven: A Comprehensive Guide to Everything the Bible Says about Our Eternal Home* (Wheaton: Tyndale House Publishers, Inc., 2004), 61.

4. Rodney Stark, *The Victory of Reason: How Christianity Led to Freedom, Capitalism, and Western Success* (New York: Random House, 2007), 130.

5. Andy Crouch, *Culture Making: Recovering Our Creative Calling* (Downers Grove, IL: InterVarsity, 2013), 263.

6. Mihaly Csikszentmihalyi, *Flow: The Psychology of Optimal Experience* (New York: Harper & Row, 1990), 3.

7. Charles Walker, "Experiencing Flow: Is Doing It Together Better Than Doing It Alone?," *Journal of Positive Psychology* 5 (2010): 3–11, https://DOI.org/10.1080/17439760903271116.

8. Barna Group, *The State of Generosity: The Heart of the Giver* (Ventura, CA: Barna Group, 2022), 117.

9. Paula Forbes, "Q&A with TipsForJesus, the Mystery Mega Tippers," Eater.com, December 10, 2013, https://www.eater.com/2013/12/10 /6316463/q-a-with-tipsforjesus-the-mystery-mega-tippers.

10. Alcorn, *Heaven*, 51.

11. Paolo Uggetti, "Retracing the Histories of 'The Next Michael Jordans,'" The Ringer, May 4, 2020, https://www.theringer.com/nba

/2020/5/4/21246021/next-michael-jordan-last-dance-kobe-bryant-lebron
-james.

12. Crouch, *Culture Making*, 97.

13. John Harrison, *Spellbound: The Wonder-Filled Life of Doug Henning* (New York: BoxOffice Books, 2009), 46.

14. Dana R. Carney et al., "The Secret Lives of Liberals and Conservatives: Personality Profiles, Interaction Styles, and the Things They Leave Behind," *Political Psychology* 29, no. 6 (2008): 807–40, http://www.jstor.org/stable/20447169.

15. Stephen J. Dollinger, "Creativity and Conservatism," *Personality and Individual Differences* 43, no. 5 (2007): 10025–35.

Chapter 9 Faithful Presence in Our Communities

1. Barna Group, *The State of Your Church* (Ventura, CA: Barna Group, 2022), 119.

2. "Loyalists," The George Washington Presidential Library at Mount Vernon, accessed September 25, 2023, https://www.mountvernon.org/library/digitalhistory/digital-encyclopedia/article/loyalists/.

3. James Davison Hunter, in Christopher Benson, "Faithful Presence," *Christianity Today*, May 14, 2010, https://www.christianitytoday.com/ct/2010/may/16.33.html.

4. David Kinnaman and Gabe Lyons, *unChristian: What a New Generation Really Thinks about Christianity . . . and Why It Matters* (Grand Rapids: Baker Books, 2012), 27.

5. Tim Muehlhoff, *I Beg to Differ: Navigating Difficult Conversations with Truth and Love* (Downers Grove, IL: InterVarsity, 2014).

6. "Five Ways to Monitor the Coronavirus Outbreak," *New York Times*, April 23, 2020, https://www.nytimes.com/interactive/2020/04/23/upshot/five-ways-to-monitor-coronavirus-outbreak-us.html.

Chapter 10 Lessons Learned

1. Sheon Han, "You Can Only Maintain So Many Close Friendships," *The Atlantic*, May 20, 2021, https://www.theatlantic.com/family/archive/2021/05/robin-dunbar-explains-circles-friendship-dunbars-number/618931/.

Having guided many projects with Barna, MARK MATLOCK has provided insights into understanding younger generations, cultivating resilient disciples, and knowing the pulse of the city you are ministering in and to. Author of more than twenty books, Mark most recently coauthored *Faith for Exiles* with David Kinnaman and is currently working on *Emotionally Healthy Discipleship for Teens* with Pete Scazzero.

Mark is the principal founder of WisdomWorks, a consulting group dedicated to helping churches and faith-centered organizations leverage the transforming power of wisdom to accomplish their mission in changing times. Mark is also a senior fellow at Barna. He is a facilitator of innovation, ideas, and impact, helping people turn data and research into strategy and action. Mark has been a consultant for many national and international faith-based organizations such as Seed Company, Awana, and MOVEMENT.ORG. He is currently the Executive Director of Urbana for InterVarsity Christian Fellowship.

Mark lives in the Dallas metroplex with his wife, Jade.